wok &
stir fry

Simple Cookery

STAR FIRE

This is a Starfire book
First published in 2001

02 04 05 03

1 3 5 7 9 10 8 6 4 2

Starfire is part of
The Foundry Creative Media Company Limited
Crabtree Hall, Crabtree Lane, Fulham, London, SW6 6TY

Visit the Foundry website: www.foundry.co.uk/recipes

ISBN: 1-903817-04-8

The CIP record for this book is available from the British Library.

Printed in Italy

ACKNOWLEDGEMENTS

Authors: Catherine Atkinson, Juliet Barker, Gina Steer,
Carol Tennant, Liz Martin, Mari Mererid Williams and Elizabeth Wolf-Cohen
Editorial Consultant: Gina Steer
Project Editor: Karen Fitzpatrick
Photography: Colin Bowling, Paul Forrester and Stephen Brayne
Home Economists and Stylists: Jacqueline Bellefontaine,
Mandy Phipps, Vicki Smallwood and Penny Stephens
Design Team: Helen Courtney, Jennifer Bishop, Lucy Bradbury and Chris Herbert

All props supplied by Barbara Stewart at Surfaces

NOTE
Recipes using uncooked eggs should be avoided by infants,
the elderly, pregnant women and anyone suffering from an illness.

Special thanks to everyone involved in this book, particularly
Karen Fitzpatrick and Gina Steer.

CONTENTS

SOUPS & STARTERS

FISH & SHELLFISH

MEAT

POULTRY

RICE & NOODLES

ENTERTAINING

HYGIENE IN THE KITCHEN

It is well worth remembering that many foods can carry some form of bacteria. In most cases, the worst it will lead to is a bout of food poisoning or gastroenteritis, although for certain groups this can be more serious – the risk can be reduced or eliminated by good food hygiene and proper cooking.

Do not buy food that is past its sell-by date and do not consume any food that is past its use-by date. When buying food, use the eyes and nose. If the food looks tired, limp or a bad colour or it has a rank, acrid or simply bad smell, do not buy or eat it under any circumstances.

Do take special care when preparing raw meat and fish. A separate chopping board should be used for each; wash the knife, board and the hands thoroughly before handling or preparing any other food.

Regularly clean, defrost and clear out the refrigerator or freezer – it is worth checking the packaging to see exactly how long each product is safe to freeze.

Avoid handling food if suffering from an upset stomach as bacteria can be passed through food preparation.

Dish cloths and tea towels must be washed and changed regularly. Ideally use disposable cloths which should be replaced on a daily basis. More durable cloths should be left to soak in bleach, then washed in the washing machine on a boil wash.

Keep the hands, cooking utensils and food preparation surfaces clean and do not allow pets to climb on to any work surfaces.

BUYING

Avoid bulk buying where possible, especially fresh produce such as meat, poultry, fish, fruit and vegetables unless buying for the freezer. Fresh foods lose their nutritional value rapidly so buying a little at a time minimises loss of nutrients. It also eliminates a packed refrigerator which reduces the effectiveness of the refrigeration process.

When buying prepackaged goods such as cans or pots of cream and yogurts, check that the packaging is intact and not damaged or pierced at all. Cans should not be dented, pierced

or rusty. Check the sell-by dates even for cans and packets of dry ingredients such as flour and rice. Store fresh foods in the refrigerator as soon as possible – not in the car or the office.

When buying frozen foods, ensure that they are not heavily iced on the outside and the contents feel completely frozen. Ensure that the frozen foods have been stored in the cabinet at the correct storage level and the temperature is below -18°C/-0.4°F. Pack in cool bags to transport home and place in the freezer as soon as possible after purchase.

PREPARATION

Make sure that all work surfaces and utensils are clean and dry. Hygiene should be given priority at all times.

Separate chopping boards should be used for raw and cooked meats, fish and vegetables. Currently, a variety of good-quality plastic boards come in various designs and colours. This makes differentiating easier and the plastic has the added hygienic advantage of being washable at high temperatures in the dishwasher. (NB: If using the board for fish, first wash in cold water, then in hot to prevent odour!) Also, remember that knives and utensils should always be thoroughly cleaned after use.

When cooking, be particularly careful to keep cooked and raw food separate to avoid any contamination. It is worth washing all fruits and vegetables regardless of whether they are going to be eaten raw or lightly cooked. This rule should apply even to prewashed herbs and salads.

Do not reheat food more than once. If using a microwave, always check that the food is piping hot all the way through. (In theory, the food should reach 70°C/158°F and needs to be cooked at that temperature for at least three minutes to ensure that all bacteria are killed.)

All poultry must be thoroughly thawed before using, including chicken and poussin. Remove the food to be thawed from the freezer and place in a shallow dish to contain the juices. Leave the food in the refrigerator until it is completely thawed. A 1.4 kg/3 lb whole chicken will take about 26–30 hours to thaw. To speed up the process immerse the chicken in cold water. However, make sure that the water is changed regularly. When the joints can move freely and no ice crystals remain in the cavity, the bird is completely thawed.

Once thawed, remove the wrapper and pat the chicken dry. Place the chicken in a shallow dish, cover lightly and store as close to the base of the refrigerator as possible. The chicken should be cooked as soon as possible.

Some foods can be cooked from frozen including many prepacked foods such as soups, sauces, casseroles and breads. Where applicable follow the manufacturers' instructions.

Vegetables and fruits can also be cooked from frozen, but meats and fish should be thawed first. The only time food can be refrozen is when the food has been thoroughly thawed then cooked. Once the food has cooled then it can be frozen again. On such occasions the food can only be stored for one month.

All poultry and game (except for duck) must be cooked thoroughly. When cooked, the juices will run clear from the thickest part of the bird – the best area to try is usually the thigh. Other meats, like minced meat and pork should be cooked right the way through. Fish should turn opaque, be firm in texture and break easily into large flakes.

When cooking leftovers, make sure they are reheated until piping hot and that any sauce or soup reaches boiling point first.

STORING

REFRIGERATING AND FREEZING

Meat, poultry, fish, seafood and dairy products should all be refrigerated. The temperature of the refrigerator should be between 1–5°C/34–41°F while the freezer temperature should not rise above -18°C/-0.4°F.

To ensure the optimum refrigerator and freezer temperature, avoid leaving the door open for a long time. Try not to overstock the refrigerator as this reduces the airflow inside and affects the effectiveness in cooling the food within.

When refrigerating cooked food, allow it to cool down quickly and completely before refrigerating. Hot food will raise the temperature of the refrigerator and possibly affect or spoil other food stored in it.

Food within the refrigerator and freezer should always be covered. Raw and cooked food should be stored in separate parts of the refrigerator. Cooked food should be kept on the top shelves of the refrigerator, while raw meat, poultry and fish should be placed on bottom shelves to avoid drips and cross-contamination. It is recommended that eggs should be refrigerated in order to maintain their freshness and shelf life.

Take care that frozen foods are not stored in the freezer for too long. Blanched vegetables can be stored for one month; beef, lamb, poultry and pork for six months and unblanched vegetables and fruits in syrup for a year. Oily fish and sausages should be stored for three months. Dairy products can last four to six months while cakes and pastries should be kept in the freezer for three to six months.

HIGH-RISK FOODS

Certain foods may carry risks to people who are considered vulnerable such as the elderly, the ill, pregnant women, babies, young infants and those suffering from a recurring illness.

It is advisable to avoid those foods listed below which belong to a higher-risk category.

There is a slight chance that some eggs carry the bacteria salmonella. Cook the eggs until both the yolk and the white are firm to eliminate this risk. Pay particular attention to dishes and products incorporating lightly cooked or raw eggs which should be eliminated from the diet. Sauces including Hollandaise, mayonnaise, mousses, soufflés and meringues all use raw or lightly cooked eggs, as do custard-based dishes, ice creams and sorbets. These are all considered high-risk foods to the vulnerable groups mentioned above.

Certain meats and poultry also carry the potential risk of salmonella and so should be cooked thoroughly until the juices run clear and there is no pinkness left. Unpasteurised products such as milk, cheese (especially soft cheese), pâté, meat (both raw and cooked) all have the potential risk of listeria and should be avoided.

When buying seafood, buy from a reputable source which has a high turnover to ensure freshness. Fish should have bright clear eyes, shiny skin and bright pink or red gills. The fish should feel stiff to the touch, with a slight smell of sea air and iodine. The flesh of fish steaks and fillets should be translucent with no signs of discolouration. Molluscs such as scallops, clams and mussels are sold fresh and are still alive. Avoid any that are open or do not close when tapped lightly. In the same way, univalves such as cockles or winkles should withdraw back into their shells when lightly prodded. When choosing cephalopods such as squid and octopus they should have a firm flesh and pleasant sea smell.

As with all fish, whether it is shellfish or seafish, care is required when freezing it. It is imperative to check whether the fish has been frozen before. If it has been frozen, then it should not be frozen again under any circumstances.

INGREDIENTS

As the recipes in this book demonstrate, wok cooking is not confined to Chinese and Thai ingredients. It is, however, with this type of cooking that the wok is most closely associated. The most fundamental ingredients, which give these cuisines their distinctive flavours, are listed below.

BAMBOO SHOOTS

These are the young, edible shoots of some kinds of bamboo and are widely available tinned. Pale yellow with a crunchy texture, they come peeled – either whole or thickly sliced. Rinse before use and transfer any unused shoots to an airtight container and cover with fresh water. Refrigerate, changing the water daily, for up to a week.

BLACK BEANS

These small black, soya beans, also known as salted black beans, have been fermented with salt to preserve them. They have a distinctive, salty flavour and savoury aroma. Often used as a seasoning in conjunction with garlic and spring onions or ginger (as in black bean sauce), they are available either dried in bags or tinned in brine.

To use either type, rinse well before using and chop a little, if preferred. The dried beans keep indefinitely, as will the tinned beans, if kept in their liquid in an airtight container in the refrigerator.

CHILLIES

Chillies are a common ingredient in both Chinese and Thai cooking and are available in many forms. Fresh chillies are easy to find and most supermarkets usually stock a range of various types. Add chilli sparingly to food until you are familiar with each type. Your heat tolerance will gradually increase the more chilli you eat.

To prepare fresh chillies, remove the stems and then halve them lengthways. Remove the seeds and chop or slice the flesh as required. The seeds are generally hotter than the flesh, so leave them in if you like your food hot. Wash your hands, knife and chopping board thoroughly before preparing any other ingredients or touching your eyes or face.

Thai and Chinese cooks also make use of dried chillies. Normally the seeds are left in and the chillies can be used either whole, split lengthways or crushed. They can also be rehydrated in almost boiling water before use. The chillies are usually removed from the dish before serving.

CHILLI BEAN SAUCE

This is a thick sauce or paste made from soya beans, chillies and other seasonings and is usually hot and spicy. It is available in jars from supermarkets and Oriental grocers and keeps well in the refrigerator.

CHILLI SAUCE

This is a bright red, hot sauce made from chillies, vinegar, sugar and salt. It is sometimes used in cooking, but is mainly useful as a dipping sauce. It is also available as sweet chilli sauce.

COCONUT

Coconut is a very common ingredient in Thai cooking. It is available in many forms including fresh, desiccated, powdered, creamed and in tins. Recipes generally specify which type to use.

CORIANDER (CHINESE PARSLEY)

Fresh, green coriander is used extensively in Thai cooking and is one of the few fresh herbs used in Chinese cookery. The leaves resemble those of flat-leaf parsley and the two are easily confused, although coriander has a much more pungent flavour and aroma. Coriander is often sold in bunches with the roots still attached. The roots are also often used in Thai recipes, especially for curry pastes. Coriander seeds are used whole or ground and are also most often used to make curry pastes.

CORNFLOUR

Cornflour is a very common thickening agent in Chinese cooking, but is also used in marinades to coat food and protect it during deep-frying. To create a sauce with a velvety texture, mix the cornflour with a little water until smooth, then add to the sauce in the wok and heat gently, stirring throughout.

FISH SAUCE

This is the basic savoury flavour in Thai cooking for which there is no substitute. It is made from fermented fish or seafood and imparts a very distinctive, salty flavour. Fish sauce is readily available in large super-markets and Oriental grocers.

GARLIC

Both Chinese and Thai cuisine rely on garlic as an essential seasoning. It is used in many forms. It is often pickled or used to flavour oils and sauces and is often paired with other pungent ingredients such as spring onions, ginger, and black beans. Look for firm, pinkish garlic and store in a cool, dry place.

GINGER AND GALANGAL

Fresh root ginger is an indispensable ingredient in Chinese cooking, although it is also used in some Thai dishes. Root ginger has a pungent, fresh, spicy fragrance and adds a subtle, hot flavour to dishes. Galangal is similar, but is more often used in Thai cooking.

HOISIN SAUCE

This is a thick, brownish-red sauce made from soya beans, vinegar, sugar and spices. It is sweet and spicy and is widely used in Chinese cookery. It is probably best known as an accompaniment to Peking Duck. It should keep indefinitely in the refrigerator.

KAFFIR LIME LEAVES

The dark green, glossy leaves of the Kaffir lime impart a unique, lemon-lime flavour to Thai cooking. They are used whole in soups and stews or finely sliced in stir-fried dishes. They are readily available in Oriental grocers and some supermarkets. Buy a large bunch and freeze in polythene bags – they will keep indefinitely. They are also available dried, but are less pungent this way.

LEMON GRASS

A common Thai ingredient, lemon grass looks a little like the spring onion. It is much tougher, however, and has a pungent lemony flavour (but lemon is not a good substitute). To use lemon grass, trim the ends, remove the toughest outer leaves and chop finely.

OIL

Oil is the most common cooking medium in wok cookery, although other fats can be used. The most common oil to use is groundnut (or peanut) oil. It is virtually tasteless and has a high smoke point, making it ideal for both stir-frying and deep-frying. Other suitable oils include safflower, sunflower and corn oil. Do not use olive oil or nut oils for stir-frying, as they have a tendency to burn at low temperatures.

Sesame oil is a thick, rich, pungent oil made from toasted sesame seeds. In Chinese cooking, it is used as a seasoning and is added after cooking. It heats very quickly and burns very easily, making it unsuitable for cooking.

RICE VINEGAR

There are several types of rice vinegar, ranging in flavour from spicy and slightly tart to sweet and pungent. White rice vinegar is the most common and is clear and mild in flavour. It is used for sweet and sour dishes. Black rice vinegar is dark in colour. It is rich yet mild in flavour and is used in braised dishes and sauces. Red rice vinegar is sweet and spicy and is usually used as a dipping sauce for seafood.

RICE WINE

L ook for Shaoxing or Shaoxing-style rice wine as it has a rich, mellow flavour that is unique. A reasonable substitute is dry sherry; it is not expensive and keeps well in the store cupboard.

SOY SAUCE

T he most essential ingredient in Chinese cooking, soy sauce is made from a mixture of soya beans, flour and water which is then fermented and aged for some months. The liquid which is finally distilled is soy sauce. There are two main types: light soy sauce and dark soy sauce. Light soy sauce, which is light in colour but very flavourful, is best for cooking. (It is saltier than dark soy sauce.) Dark soy sauce is aged for longer than light soy sauce and has a darker, almost black colour. It is slightly thicker and stronger than light soy sauce and is generally used as a dipping sauce. Japanese soy sauce is also very dark, but has a more rounded flavour, while still being salty.

TAMARIND

A useful sour flavour in Thai cooking, tamarind is usually available in compressed blocks from Oriental and Asian grocers. To extract the juice or water, mix the pulp with double the amount of hot water then press through a sieve. Discard the seeds.

TOFU

T ofu is also known by its Chinese name *doufu*. It is an important ingredient in both Thai and Chinese cuisines and is highly nutritious, being rich in protein. It has a distinctive texture but very bland flavour. It is made from yellow soya beans that have been soaked, ground, mixed with water and then cooked briefly before being solidified. It is sold in several forms; some varieties are coarse-textured, whereas others are silky and smooth. The coarser type is useful for stir-frying, while the silky type is often used in soups.

Tofu is usually sold packed in water. Once opened, store in the refrigerator for up to five days, changing the water daily. To use solid tofu, drain it well by pressing between sheets of absorbent kitchen paper and then cut into cubes or shreds. Cook it carefully as too much handling will cause it to disintegrate.

EQUIPMENT AND TECHNIQUES

T here are numerous pieces of equipment that are very useful for stir-frying. Most can be bought very cheaply from Oriental grocers, or often more expensively from department stores.

EQUIPMENT

WOK

The most useful piece of equipment is, of course, the wok. It is much easier to use than a frying pan because of its depth, making it easier to toss the food around quickly without spilling it. A wok also requires a lot less oil for deep-frying than a deep-fat fryer, although more care is required in terms of safety. Another advantage is that the shape of the wok allows heat to spread more evenly, ensuring that the food cooks much more quickly.

There are a number of shapes of wok available. The Cantonese wok has short handles on each side. This type of wok is best for steaming and deep-frying because it is easier to move when full of liquid. The Pau wok has a single handle and is better for stir-frying, allowing you to manoeuvre the pan with one hand while stirring the food with the other one.

Woks can also have rounded or slightly flattened bases. Round-bottomed woks are really only suitable for use on gas hobs. Flattened-bottomed woks can be used on gas and electric hobs but are better for deep-frying than stir-frying.

When choosing a wok, look for a large one simply because it is easier to cook a small amount in a large wok than a large amount in a small one. Choose a wok that is heavy and made of carbon steel, rather than stainless steel or aluminium, which tend to scorch. Non-stick woks are also available but these cannot be seasoned or used over very high temperatures, both of which are essential for flavour in stir-frying. Electric woks are also available, but these cannot be heated sufficiently hot enough and tend to have very shallow sides. They also lack the manoeuvrability of a free-standing wok.

If you buy a carbon-steel wok, it will need to be seasoned before use. First, scrub well using a cream cleanser or another abrasive to remove the machine oil with which it will probably have been coated to prevent rusting. Dry it well and then place it over a low heat. Add a little cooking oil and rub this all over the cooking surface with wadded kitchen paper. Continue heating over a low heat for 10–15 minutes, then wipe well with more kitchen paper – the paper will blacken. Repeat this process of coating, heating and wiping until the kitchen paper comes away clean. With continued use, the wok will darken further.

Do not scrub a seasoned wok with soap and water. Wash in hot, plain water using a brush or non-stick scrubber. Dry thoroughly with absorbent kitchen paper and place over a low heat until completely dry. Rub with a few drops of cooking oil to prevent rusting. If a little rust does appear, scrub off with cream cleanser or another abrasive and repeat the seasoning process.

ACCESSORIES

If your hob will not support a free-standing wok, Oriental stores sell metal rings or frames, called wok stands, that stabilize round-bottomed woks. These stands are an essential piece of equipment, so if you plan on doing a lot of steaming, deep-frying or braising in your wok it may be worth purchasing one. The stands are available in two designs: one is a solid ring punched with ventilation holes and the other is a circular wire frame. Only use the wire frame stand if you have a gas hob as the other stand will not allow sufficient ventilation.

You may also find it useful to have a lid for your wok. Wok lids are dome-like in shape, are usually made from aluminium and are very inexpensive. Any large, dome-shaped pan lid that fits snugly over the wok will suffice. Alternatively, use kitchen foil.

A long-handled spatula is also an important piece of equipment. Special spatulas with rounded ends are readily available and make stirring and tossing food in the wok much easier. A long-handled spoon can be used instead.

If you are going to use the wok as a steamer, a wooden or metal rack or trivet is also a useful tool, as it holds the plate or steamer above the water.

Chinese cooks would not be without a cleaver. It differs from a meat cleaver in that a Chinese cleaver has a finer, much sharper blade and is used for all kinds of cutting, from shredding to chopping up bones. Several types of Chinese cleavers are available including a light-weight, narrow-bladed cleaver for cutting delicate foods such as vegetables, a medium-weight model for general use and a heavy cleaver for heavy-duty chopping.

For steaming, it may be worth investing in a bamboo steamer. They are both attractive and effective. They come in a variety of sizes and stack together with the uppermost basket having a lid. Fill the steamer with food, placing the food needing the longest cooking time in the bottom basket and the more delicate foods in the top basket. Stand the steamer on a trivet in a steady wok of boiling water. Cover tightly and leave to cook.

Another useful piece of equipment if you plan to do a lot of cooking in the wok is an electric rice cooker. It will cook rice perfectly and keep it warm, sometimes up to several hours. It also has the advantage of freeing-up cooker space. They are relatively expensive, however, but if you cook rice frequently it may be worth buying.

Chopsticks are used in Chinese and Japanese cookery not just for eating but for stirring, beating and whipping. They are available in wood and plastic and can be bought in Oriental grocers and department stores. Chinese chopsticks are larger with blunted ends, while Japanese chopsticks tend to be smaller with pointed ends.

To use chopsticks, put one chopstick into the crook of your preferred hand, between your thumb and first finger, holding the chopstick about two-thirds of the way up from the thinner end. Let it rest on your third finger. Put the second chopstick between your thumb and fore-finger so that its tip is level with the chopstick below. Keep the lower chopstick steady and move the top one to pick up food.

TECHNIQUES

The initial preparation of food in wok cooking is probably more important than the cooking itself. Most dishes are cooked very rapidly, so it is important that everything is prepared beforehand and is chopped into small, even-sized pieces to ensure quick, even cooking without overcooking. This type of preparation also ensures the dish looks attractive.

Wok cookery covers a number of different cooking methods – sometimes in one recipe – and most are easily mastered. When planning a meal, make sure you select dishes using different cooking methods and only one that is stir-fried.

CUTTING TECHNIQUES

SLICING Several different types of slicing methods are useful in wok and stir-fry cooking, including the conventional method of laying the food firmly on a chopping board and slicing straight down to cut the food into thin slices. Meat is always sliced across the grain to break up the fibres and to make it more tender when cooked. If you use a cleaver, hold the cleaver with your index finger over the far side of the top of the cleaver and your thumb on the side nearest to you and guide the cutting edge firmly through the food. With your other hand, hold the food and make sure when cutting that you turn your fingers under for safety.

CHOPPING This is the simplest technique and refers to simply cutting food through. With whole birds or cooked food with bones which needs to be chopped into smaller pieces, place on a firm surface, then using a straight, sharp, downward motion, chop through the bones, hitting down with the blade, then finish off the blow with the flat of your other hand on the top edge of the knife or cleaver. A heavy cleaver or knife is best for these tasks.

DIAGONAL SLICING This is particularly useful for vegetables as it exposes more surface area to the heat of the wok and also makes the food look much more interesting. Simply angle the knife or cleaver against the food and slice. For larger vegetables such as courgettes, carrots and aubergines, make one diagonal cut at the end of the vegetable. Turn the vegetable 90 degrees, cut in half lengthways, then diagonally slice each half. Continue until the whole vegetable has been chopped into even-sized pieces.

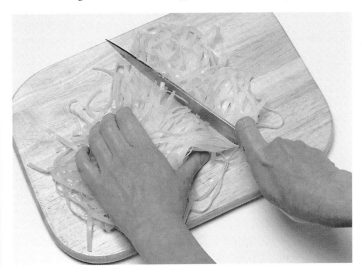

DICING This is a simple technique of cutting food into small cubes or dice. First cut the food into slices as for shredding. Stack the slices and slice again lengthways into sticks, again as you would for shredding. Turn the sticks again and cut crossways into cubes.

HORIZONTAL OR FLAT SLICING

This is a technique for slicing whole foods thinly, while retaining the overall shape. A cleaver is particularly useful for this technique. Hold the knife or cleaver with the blade parallel to the chopping board. Place your free hand on top of the food to be sliced. Using a gentle slicing motion, slice sideways into the food and right the way through, taking care to keep your upper hand out of the way. This is particularly useful for splitting chicken breasts and similar meats.

MINCING This is a very fine chopping technique. First slice the food and then chop it rapidly – it will spread out over the chopping area. Gather it into a pile and continue chopping and regathering until the food is chopped as finely as needed. If very fine results are required, a food processor may be a better tool to use, but be careful not to overprocess.

SCORING This is used to score the surface of foods, such as duck breasts and squid to help them cook faster and evenly and to give them an attractive appearance. Use a cleaver or sharp knife and make shallow cuts into the food at a slight angle. Take care not to cut all the way through. Make cuts right across the food, then turn and make a second series of cuts at an angle to the first set to make diamond shapes.

SHREDDING This is cutting food into fine, matchstick shreds. First cut the food into slices, then stack the slices and cut again, lengthways this time, into fine shreds. It is sometimes easier to cut meat and fish if they have been placed in the freezer for 20–30 minutes before slicing.

OTHER USEFUL TECHNIQUES

MARINATING This is a common process in Chinese and other Oriental cookery to add flavour to meat, fish and vegetables. The food is steeped in a mixture of flavours, which could include soy sauce, rice wine, garlic, ginger or spices. Marinating time is usually at least 20 minutes, but often can be as long as overnight. Food is usually removed from the marinade before cooking.

THICKENING There are two useful ways of thickening sauces. The first is to use cornflour mixed until smooth with a little water that is then whisked into the hot, not boiling, sauce. The sauce is brought up to the simmer and cooked gently for about 2 minutes until thickened. The other method of thickening is to reduce the sauce; the liquid is simmered until most of the excess liquid has boiled off, leaving a concentrated and thickened sauce.

VELVETING This is a particularly useful technique in Chinese cooking which helps to protect delicate foods, such as chicken breasts, from overcooking. The food is coated with a mixture of cornflour and egg white and sometimes salt. The mixture is marinated in the refrigerator for 20–30 minutes before cooking.

COOKING TECHNIQUES

BLANCHING This method involves cooking food in boiling water or moderately hot oil for a few minutes so that it is partly cooked, which speeds up the cooking process later on, so that other elements of the dish do not overcook. Chicken is often blanched in oil after velveting, meat is often blanched in water to remove excess fat and vegetables are often blanched in water, drained and refreshed under cold water, before being drained again and dried. In the case of vegetables, stir-frying merely heats them through and finishes the cooking.

BRAISING This is a method often applied to tougher cuts of meat that need long, slow cooking times to remain moist. The food is usually browned and then cooked in stock or liquid to which other flavourings are also added. The mixture is brought up to simmering point and then cooked gently until tender.

DEEP-FRYING This is another very important technique in Far Eastern cookery. Woks are very useful for deep-frying as they use far less oil than conventional deep-fat fryers. Although a deep-fat fryer is safer, a few precautions mean that deep-frying in a wok is very easy. Ensure that the wok sits securely on the hob, either by using a flat-bottomed wok or a wok stand. Carefully add the oil, ensuring that the wok is no more than half full. Heat up slowly to the required temperature.

To test for temperature, either use a thermometer made for the purpose or the following test. Add a small cube of crustless bread and time how long it takes to brown. Generally, if the bread browns in 30 seconds, the oil is at the correct temperature. If it browns more quickly the oil is too hot. If it takes longer to brown the oil is too cold. Allow the oil to return to the correct temperature between batches of food and do not overfill the wok. Do not leave the wok unsupervised on the stove when deep frying.

It is also important that food to be deep-fried is dry. Lift food from a marinade and blot thoroughly on kitchen paper. If using batter, allow any excess to drip off before adding to the oil.

Oil used for deep-frying can be reused. Allow the oil to cool completely and then strain into a clean jar or other container. Label the jar with the type of food the oil was used for and only reuse it for the same type of food. Oil can be reused up to 3 times.

POACHING This is a method of cooking meat or fish in simmering liquid until nearly cooked so that it can be added to soup or combined with a sauce to finish the cooking.

SHALLOW-FRYING This is similar to sautéing as it involves more oil than stir-frying, but less than deep-frying. Food is fried first on one side and then on the other. Often the excess oil is drained off and a sauce is made in the same pan. A frying pan is preferable for shallow-frying rather than a wok.

SLOW-SIMMERING AND STEEPING Slow-simmered food is cooked very gently in liquid that just simmers. Simmering is the method for making stock. Steeping is a similar method, except that the heat is turned off and the heat of the liquid alone finishes off the cooking process.

STEAMING Steaming is an ancient technique currently enjoying a revival because it adds no fat to the food being cooked. Steamed foods are cooked on a gentle, moist heat. Steaming is particularly suited to vegetable and fish.

Woks can be used as steamers in two ways. The first method is described under the section on bamboo steamers. The second method involves putting about 5 cm/2 inches of water in a stable wok on the hob. A metal or wooden rack or trivet is then placed into the wok and the water is brought to the boil. The food to be steamed should be arranged on a plate and the plate should be lowered on to the rack. The wok then needs to be covered tightly with a lid. For longer cooking times, the water may need replenishing.

STIR-FRYING This is the most famous of wok cooking techniques and is used throughout China and the Far East as well as in India. It is possibly the most tricky of wok techniques because it involves a lot of preparation as well as a good source of heat. Its advantage is that stir-fried foods can be cooked very quickly in very little oil so that they retain their colour, flavour and texture. It is very important that stir-fried foods are not greasy or overcooked.

STEPS TO STIR-FRYING (ONCE ALL THE INGREDIENTS ARE PREPARED AND TO HAND):

- Heat the wok or frying pan over the highest heat until it is very hot before adding the oil. This prevents the food from sticking and ensures an even heat. Add the oil and using a spatula or long-handled spoon, distribute it evenly over the surface. It should be very hot – almost smoking – before you add any ingredients (unless you are adding flavouring ingredients). If you are flavouring the oil, for example with garlic, ginger, spring onions or chilli (or a combination) do not let the oil become smoking hot because these types of ingredients

will burn at such high temperatures and become bitter. Add to hot but not smoking oil and toss the ingredients around quickly for a few seconds. In some recipes these ingredients are removed and discarded.

- Now add the next ingredients as described in the recipe and proceed to stir-fry by tossing quickly in the wok using a spatula or long-handled spoon. When cooking meat, allow it to rest for a few seconds between stirring it. Otherwise keep the food moving, transferring it from the bottom to the sides of the wok and back again. Because of the high heat involved when stir-frying, there may be some spluttering and splattering of hot fat, so take care during this stage of cooking.

- Once everything is cooked, some stir-fried dishes are thickened with a mixture of cornflour and water. To avoid a lumpy sauce, make sure the mixture is smooth and reduce the heat to just below simmering point before adding it. Stir in the cornflour mixture then increase the heat to a simmer and cook for a further 2–3 minutes, until the sauce is thickened, smooth and coats all the ingredients.

TWICE-COOKING As the name implies, this is a two-step process involving two different techniques, such as simmering and stir-frying. For example, pork ribs may be gently simmered to remove the excess fat before draining and stir-frying or braising with other flavours.

GARNISHES

Oriental cuisines pay a lot of attention to the finished appearance of food and this is one reason for cutting ingredients carefully. Often dishes will be garnished attractively with anything from simple shredded chillies to more elaborate spring onion tassels. Thai cooks often go to elaborate lengths, carving flowers from carrots or making tomato roses as garnishes. In fact, the Thai Royal family employs an official Fruit Carver (a hereditary post) for special occasions. The home cook can create some simple effects with everyday ingredients and a sharp knife.

CHILLI FLOWERS Take a well-formed red chilli, about 5–7.5 cm/2–3 inches long, with the stem intact. Hold the chilli by the stem and, using a fine sharp knife, cut from the tip to the stem, at equal distances all the way around, without cutting through the stem. Try to leave the seeds intact. Gently pull back the strips and drop into iced water. The strips will curl back into a flower.

SPRING ONION TASSELS Trim the top green end of a spring onion and cut a piece about 5–7.5 cm/2–3 inches long, including about 1 cm/½ inch of the white base. With a fine, sharp knife, and holding the white part as a base, shred the green part as finely as possible. Drop into a bowl of iced water until the shreds curl back.

WONTON SOUP

INGREDIENTS   Serves 6

FOR THE CHICKEN STOCK:
900 g/2 lb chicken or chicken
  pieces with back, feet and
  wings
1–2 onions, peeled and
  quartered
2 carrots, peeled and chopped
2 celery stalks, trimmed and
  chopped
1 leek, trimmed and chopped
2 garlic cloves, unpeeled and
  lightly crushed
1 tbsp black peppercorns
2 bay leaves
small bunch parsley, stems
  only

2–3 slices fresh root ginger,
  peeled (optional)
3.4 litres/6 pints cold water

FOR THE SOUP:
18 wontons
2–3 Chinese leaves, or a
  handful of spinach, shredded
1 small carrot, peeled and cut
  into matchsticks
2–4 spring onions, trimmed
  and diagonally sliced
soy sauce, to taste
handful flat-leaf parsley, to
  garnish

1 Chop the duck into 6–8 pieces and put into a large stock pot or saucepan of water with the remaining stock ingredients. Place over a high heat and bring to the boil, skimming off any scum which rises to the surface. Reduce the heat and simmer for 2–3 hours, skimming occasionally.

2 Strain the stock through a fine sieve or muslin-lined sieve into a large bowl. Leave to cool, then chill in the refrigerator for 5–6 hours, or overnight. When cold, skim off the fat and remove any small pieces of fat by dragging a piece of absorbent kitchen paper lightly across the surface.

3 Bring a medium saucepan of water to the boil. Add the wontons and return to the boil. Simmer for 2–3 minutes, or until the wontons are cooked, stir frequently. Rinse under cold running water, drain and reserve.

4 Pour 300 ml/½ pint stock per person into a large wok. Bring to the boil over a high heat, skimming any foam that rises to the surface and simmer for 5–7 minutes to reduce slightly. Add the wontons, Chinese leaves or spinach, carrots and spring onions. Season with a few drops of soy sauce and simmer for 2–3 minutes. Garnish with a few parsley leaves and serve immediately.

THAI HOT-&-SOUR PRAWN SOUP

INGREDIENTS
Serves 6

700 g/1½ lb large raw prawns
2 tbsp vegetable oil
3–4 stalks lemon grass, outer
   leaves discarded and
   coarsely chopped
2.5 cm/1 inch piece fresh root
   ginger, peeled and finely
   chopped
2–3 garlic cloves, peeled and
   crushed
small bunch fresh coriander,
   leaves stripped and
   reserved, stems finely
   chopped

½ tsp freshly ground black
   pepper
1.8 litres/3¼ pints water
1–2 small red chillies,
   deseeded and thinly sliced
1–2 small green chillies,
   deseeded and thinly sliced
6 kaffir lime leaves, thinly
   shredded
4 spring onions, trimmed and
   diagonally sliced
1–2 tbsp Thai fish sauce
1–2 tbsp freshly squeezed lime
   juice

1 Remove the heads from the prawns by twisting away from the body and reserve. Peel the prawns, leaving the tails on and reserve the shells with the heads. Using a sharp knife, remove the black vein from the back of the prawns. Rinse and dry the prawns and reserve. Rinse and dry the heads and shells.

2 Heat a wok, add the oil and, when hot, add the prawn heads and shells, the lemon grass, ginger, garlic, coriander stems and black pepper and stir-fry for 2–3 minutes, or until the prawn heads and shells turn pink and all the ingredients are coloured.

3 Carefully add the water to the wok and return to the boil, skimming off any scum which rises to the surface. Simmer over a medium heat for 10 minutes or until slightly reduced. Strain through a fine sieve and return the clear prawn stock to the wok.

4 Bring the stock back to the boil and add the reserved prawns, chillies, lime leaves and spring onions and simmer for 3 minutes, or until the prawns turn pink. Season with the fish sauce and lime juice. Spoon into heated soup bowls, dividing the prawns evenly and float a few coriander leaves over the surface.

FOOD FACT

Thai fish sauce, made from fermented anchovies, has a sour, salty, fishy flavour.

CREAMY CARIBBEAN CHICKEN & COCONUT SOUP

INGREDIENTS   Serves 4

6–8 spring onions
2 garlic cloves
1 red chilli
175 g/6 oz cooked chicken,
  shredded or diced
2 tbsp vegetable oil
1 tsp ground turmeric
300 ml/½ pint coconut
  milk
900 ml/1½ pints chicken stock

50 g/2 oz small soup pasta or
  spaghetti, broken into small
  pieces
½ lemon, sliced
salt and freshly ground black
  pepper
1–2 tbsp freshly chopped
  coriander
sprigs of fresh coriander, to
  garnish

1 Trim the spring onions and thinly slice; peel the garlic and finely chop. Cut off the top from the chilli, slit down the side and remove seeds and membrane, then finely chop and reserve.

2 Remove and discard any skin or bones from the cooked chicken and shred using 2 forks and reserve.

3 Heat a large wok, add the oil and when hot add the spring onions, garlic and chilli and stir-fry for 2 minutes, or until the onion has softened. Stir in the turmeric and cook for 1 minute.

4 Blend the coconut milk with the chicken stock until smooth, then pour into the wok. Add the pasta or spaghetti with the lemon slices and bring to the boil.

5 Simmer, half-covered, for 10–12 minutes, or until the pasta is tender; stir occasionally.

6 Remove the lemon slices from the wok and add the chicken. Season to taste with salt and pepper and simmer for 2–3 minutes, or until the chicken is heated through thoroughly.

7 Stir in the chopped coriander and ladle into heated bowls. Garnish with sprigs of fresh coriander and serve immediately.

HELPFUL HINT

Be careful handling chillies. Either wear rubber gloves or scrub your hands thoroughly, using plenty of soap and water. Avoid touching eyes or any other sensitive areas.

SWEETCORN & CRAB SOUP

INGREDIENTS   Serves 4

450 g/1 lb fresh corn-on-
  the-cob
1.3 litres/2¼ pints chicken stock
2–3 spring onions, trimmed
  and finely chopped
1 cm/½ inch piece fresh root
  ginger, peeled and finely
  chopped
1 tbsp dry sherry or Chinese
  rice wine
2–3 tsp soy sauce

1 tsp soft light brown sugar
salt and freshly ground black
  pepper
2 tsp cornflour
225 g/8 oz white crabmeat,
  fresh or canned
1 medium egg white
1 tsp sesame oil
1–2 tbsp freshly chopped
  coriander

1 Wash the corns cobs and dry. Using a sharp knife and holding the corn cobs at an angle to the cutting board, cut down along the cobs to remove the kernels, then scrape the cobs to remove any excess milky residue. Put the kernels and the milky residue into a large wok.

2 Add the chicken stock to the wok and place over a high heat. Bring to the boil, stirring and pressing some of the kernels against the side of the wok to squeeze out the starch to help thicken the soup. Simmer for 15 minutes, stirring occasionally.

3 Add the spring onions, ginger, sherry or Chinese rice wine, soy sauce and brown sugar to the wok and season to taste with salt and pepper. Simmer for a further 5 minutes, stirring occasionally.

4 Blend the cornflour with 1 tablespoon of cold water to form a smooth paste and whisk into the soup. Return to the boil, then simmer over medium heat until thickened.

5 Add the crabmeat, stirring until blended. Beat the egg white with the sesame oil and stir into the soup in a slow steady stream, stirring constantly. Stir in the chopped coriander and serve immediately.

TASTY TIP

For chicken stock that is homemade, follow the instructions for Wonton Soup (see page 16).

HOT-&-SOUR SOUP

INGREDIENTS   Serves 4–6

25 g/1 oz dried Chinese
(shiitake) mushrooms
2 tbsp groundnut oil
1 carrot, peeled and cut
into julienne strips
125 g/4 oz chestnut
mushrooms, wiped and
thinly sliced
2 garlic cloves, peeled and
finely chopped
½ tsp dried crushed chillies
1.1 litres/2 pints chicken stock
(see page 16)
75 g/3 oz cooked boneless
chicken or pork, shredded

125 g/4 oz fresh bean curd,
thinly sliced, optional
2–3 spring onions, trimmed
and finely sliced diagonally
1–2 tsp sugar
3 tbsp cider vinegar
2 tbsp soy sauce
salt and freshly ground black
pepper
1 tbsp cornflour
1 large egg
2 tsp sesame oil
2 tbsp freshly chopped
coriander

1 Place the dried Chinese (shiitake) mushrooms in a small bowl and pour over enough almost boiling water to cover. Leave for 20 minutes to soften, then gently lift out and squeeze out the liquid. (Lifting out the mushrooms leaves any sand and grit behind.) Discard the stems and thinly slice the caps and reserve.

2 Heat a large wok, add the oil and when hot, add the carrot strips and stir-fry for 2–3 minutes, or until beginning to soften. Add the chestnut mushrooms and stir-fry for 2–3 minutes, or until golden, then stir in the garlic and chillies.

3 Add the chicken stock to the vegetables and bring to the

boil, skimming any foam which rises to the surface. Add the shredded chicken or pork, bean curd, if using, spring onions, sugar, vinegar, soy sauce and reserved Chinese mushrooms and simmer for 5 minutes, stirring occasionally. Season to taste with salt and pepper.

4 Blend the cornflour with 1 tablespoon of cold water to form a smooth paste and whisk into the soup. Return to the boil and simmer over a medium heat until thickened.

5 Beat the egg with the sesame oil and slowly add to the soup in a slow, steady stream, stirring constantly. Stir in the chopped coriander and serve the soup immediately.

CHINESE LEAF & MUSHROOM SOUP

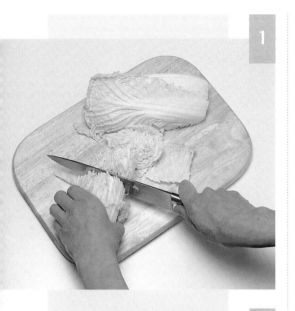

INGREDIENTS   Serves 4–6

450 g/1 lb Chinese leaves
25 g/1 oz dried Chinese
  (shiitake) mushrooms
1 tbsp vegetable oil
75 g/3 oz smoked streaky
  bacon, diced
2.5 cm/1 inch piece fresh root
  ginger, peeled and finely
  chopped
175 g/6 oz chestnut
  mushrooms, thinly sliced

1.1 litres/2 pints chicken stock
4–6 spring onions, trimmed
  and cut into short lengths
2 tbsp dry sherry or Chinese
  rice wine
salt and freshly ground black
  pepper
sesame oil for drizzling

1 Trim the stem ends of the Chinese leaves and cut in half lengthways. Remove the triangular core with a knife, then cut into 2.5 cm/1 inch slices and reserve.

2 Place the dried Chinese mushrooms in a bowl and pour over enough almost boiling water to cover. Leave to stand for 20 minutes to soften, then gently lift out and squeeze out the liquid. Discard the stems and thinly slice the caps and reserve. Strain the liquid through a muslin-lined sieve or a coffee filter paper and reserve.

3 Heat a wok over a medium-high heat, add the oil and when hot add the bacon. Stir-fry for 3–4 minutes, or until crisp and golden, stirring frequently. Add the ginger and chestnut mushrooms and stir-fry for a further 2–3 minutes.

4 Add the chicken stock and bring to the boil, skimming any fat and scum that rises to the surface. Add the spring onions, sherry or rice wine, Chinese leaves, sliced Chinese mushrooms and season to taste with salt and pepper. Pour in the reserved soaking liquid and reduce the heat to the lowest possible setting.

5 Simmer gently, covered, until all the vegetables are very tender; this will take about 10 minutes. Add a little water if the liquid has reduced too much. Spoon into soup bowls and drizzle with a little sesame oil. Serve immediately.

TASTY TIP

If Chinese leaves are not available, use Savoy cabbage.

VIETNAMESE BEEF & RICE NOODLE SOUP

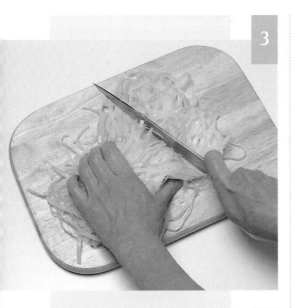

INGREDIENTS   Serves 4–6

FOR THE BEEF STOCK:
900 g/2 lb meaty beef bones
1 large onion, peeled and
  quartered
2 carrots, peeled and cut
  into chunks
2 celery stalks, trimmed and
  sliced
1 leek, washed and sliced
  into chunks
2 garlic cloves, unpeeled and
  lightly crushed
3 whole star anise
1 tsp black peppercorns

FOR THE SOUP:
175 g/6 oz dried rice stick
  noodles
4–6 spring onions, trimmed
  and diagonally sliced
1 red chilli, deseeded and
  diagonally sliced
1 small bunch fresh
  coriander
1 small bunch fresh mint
350 g/12 oz fillet steak, very
  thinly sliced
salt and freshly ground black
  pepper

1 Place all the ingredients for the beef stock into a large stock pot or saucepan and cover with cold water. Bring to the boil and skim off any scum that rises to the surface. Reduce the heat and simmer gently, partially covered, for 2–3 hours, skimming occasionally.

2 Strain into a large bowl and leave to cool, then skim off the fat. Chill in the refrigerator and when cold remove any fat from the surface. Pour 1.7 litres/ 3 pints of the stock into a large wok and reserve.

3 Cover the noodles with warm water and leave for 3 minutes, or until just softened. Drain, then cut into 10 cm/4 inch lengths.

4 Arrange the spring onions and chilli on a serving platter or large plate. Strip the leaves from the coriander and mint and arrange them in piles on the plate.

5 Bring the stock in the wok to the boil over a high heat. Add the noodles and simmer for about 2 minutes, or until tender. Add the beef strips and simmer for about 1 minute. Season to taste with salt and pepper.

6 Ladle the soup with the noodles and beef strips into individual soup bowls and serve immediately with the plate of condiments handed around separately.

LAKSA MALAYAN RICE NOODLE SOUP

INGREDIENTS   Serves 4–6

1.1 kg/2½ lb corn-fed, free-
  range chicken
1 tsp black peppercorns
1 tbsp vegetable oil
1 large onion, peeled and
  thinly sliced
2 garlic cloves, peeled and
  finely chopped
2.5 cm/1 inch piece fresh root
  ginger, peeled and thinly
  sliced
1 tsp ground coriander
2 red chillies, deseeded and
  diagonally sliced

1–2 tsp hot curry paste
400 ml/14 fl oz coconut milk
450 g/1 lb large raw prawns,
  peeled and deveined
½ small head of Chinese
  leaves, thinly shredded
1 tsp sugar
2 spring onions, trimmed and
  thinly sliced
125 g/4 oz beansprouts
250 g/9 oz rice noodles or rice
  sticks, soaked as per packet
  instructions
fresh mint leaves, to garnish

1 Put the chicken in a
large saucepan with the
peppercorns and cover with
cold water. Bring to the boil,
skimming off any scum that
rises to the surface. Simmer,
partially covered, for about
1 hour. Remove the chicken
and cool. Skim any fat from
the stock and strain through
a muslin-lined sieve and reserve.
Remove the meat from the
carcass, shred and reserve.

2 Heat a large wok, add
the oil and when hot,
add the onions and stir-fry
for 2 minutes, or until they
begin to colour. Stir in the
garlic, ginger, coriander, chillies
and curry paste and stir-fry for
a further 2 minutes.

3 Carefully pour in the reserved
stock (you need at least 1.1
litres/2 pints) and simmer gently,
partially covered, for 10 minutes,
or until slightly reduced.

4 Add the coconut milk,
prawns, Chinese leaves, sugar,
spring onions and beansprouts
and simmer for 3 minutes, stirring
occasionally. Add the reserved
shredded chicken, and cook for
a further 2 minutes.

5 Drain the noodles and divide
between 4–6 soup bowls.
Ladle the hot stock and vegetables
over the noodles, making sure
each serving has some prawns
and chicken. Garnish each bowl
with fresh mint leaves and serve
immediately.

WOK-FRIED SNACKS – POPCORN & SESAME-COATED PECANS

INGREDIENTS — Serves 4–6

FOR THE POPCORN:
75 ml/ 3 fl oz vegetable oil
75 g/3 oz unpopped popcorn
½ tsp garlic salt
1 tsp hot chilli powder

FOR THE PECANS:
50 g/2 oz sugar
½ tsp ground cinnamon

½ tsp ground Chinese five
    spice powder
¼ tsp salt
¼ tsp cayenne pepper
175 g/6 oz pecan or walnut
    halves
sesame seeds for sprinkling

1 For the popcorn, heat half the oil in a large wok over a medium-high heat. Add 2–3 kernels and cover with a lid. When these kernels pop, add all the popcorn and cover tightly. Cook until the popping stops, shaking from time to time.

2 When the popping stops, pour the popped corn into a bowl and immediately add the remaining oil to the wok with the garlic salt and chilli powder. Stir-fry for 30 seconds, or until blended and fragrant.

3 Return the popcorn to the wok, stir-fry and toss for a further 30 seconds, or until coated. Pour into the bowl and serve warm or at room temperature.

4 For the pecans, put the sugar, cinnamon, Chinese five spice powder, salt and cayenne pepper into a large wok

and stir in 50 ml/2 fl oz water. Bring to the boil over a high heat, then simmer for 4 minutes, stirring frequently.

5 Remove from the heat and stir in the pecans or walnuts until well coated. Turn onto a lightly oiled, non-stick baking sheet and sprinkle generously with the sesame seeds.

6 Working quickly with 2 forks, separate the nuts into individual pieces or bite-sized clusters. Sprinkle with a few more sesame seeds and leave to cool completely. Carefully remove from the baking sheet, breaking into smaller pieces if necessary.

HELPFUL HINT

Popping corn is readily available and should be stored in an airtight container.

PRAWN TOASTS

INGREDIENTS   Serves 8–10

225 g/8 oz cooked peeled prawns, thawed if frozen, well drained and dried
1 medium egg white
2 spring onions, trimmed and chopped
1 cm/½ inch piece fresh root ginger, peeled and chopped
1 garlic clove, peeled and chopped
1 tsp cornflour

2–3 dashes hot pepper sauce
½ tsp sugar
salt and freshly ground black pepper
8 slices firm-textured white bread
4–5 tbsp sesame seeds
300 ml/½ pint vegetable oil for deep frying
sprigs of fresh coriander, to garnish

1 Put the prawns, egg white, spring onions, ginger, garlic, cornflour, hot pepper sauce and sugar into a food processor. Season to taste with about ½ teaspoon of salt and black pepper.

2 Process until the mixture forms a smooth paste, scraping down the side of the bowl once or twice.

3 Using a metal palette knife, spread an even layer of the paste evenly over the bread slices. Sprinkle each slice generously with sesame seeds, pressing gently to bury them in the paste.

4 Trim the crusts off each slice, then cut each slice diagonally into 4 triangles. Cut each triangle in half again to make 8 pieces from each slice.

5 Heat the vegetable oil in a large wok to 190°C/375°F,

or until a small cube of bread browns in about 30 seconds. Working in batches, fry the prawn triangles for 30–60 seconds, or until they are golden, turning once.

6 Remove with a slotted spoon and drain on absorbent kitchen paper. Keep the toasts warm. Arrange them on a large serving plate and garnish with sprigs of fresh coriander. Serve immediately.

TASTY TIP

This is a classic Chinese appetiser. Serve it with a selection of other snacks as a starter, or with drinks.

SESAME PRAWNS

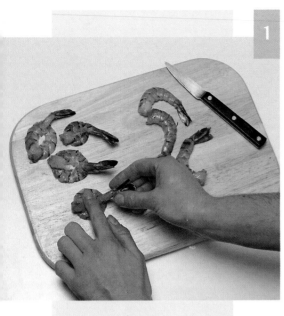

INGREDIENTS

Serves 6–8

24 large raw prawns
40 g/1 oz plain
 flour
4 tbsp sesame seeds
salt and freshly ground black
 pepper
1 large egg
300 ml/½ pint vegetable oil
 for deep frying

FOR THE SOY DIPPING SAUCE:
50 ml/2 fl oz soy sauce
1 spring onion, trimmed and
 finely chopped
½ tsp dried crushed chillies
1 tbsp sesame oil
1–2 tsp sugar, or to taste
strips of spring onion,
 to garnish

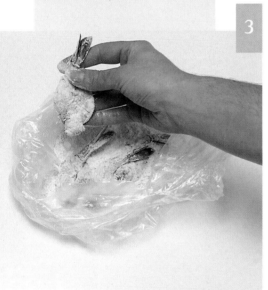

1 Remove the heads from the prawns by twisting away from the body and discard. Peel the prawns, leaving the tails on for presentation. Using a sharp knife, remove the black vein from the back of the prawns. Rinse and dry.

2 Slice along the back, but do not cut through the prawn body. Place on the chopping board and press firmly to flatten slightly, to make a butterfly shape.

3 Put the flour, half the sesame seeds, salt and pepper into a food processor and blend for 30 seconds. Tip into a polythene bag and add the prawns, 4–5 at a time. Twist to seal, then shake to coat with the flour.

4 Beat the egg in a small bowl with the remaining sesame seeds, salt and pepper.

5 Heat the oil in a large wok to 190°C/ 375°F, or until a small cube of bread browns in

about 30 seconds. Working in batches of 5 or 6, and holding each prawn by the tail, dip into the beaten egg, then carefully lower into the oil.

6 Cook for 1–2 minutes, or until crisp and golden, turning once or twice. Using a slotted spoon, remove the prawns, drain on absorbent kitchen paper and keep warm.

7 To make the dipping sauce, stir together the soy sauce, spring onion, chillies, oil and sugar until the sugar dissolves. Arrange the prawns on a plate, garnish with strips of spring onion and serve immediately.

HELPFUL HINT

Raw prawns are widely available but are cheapest bought frozen in boxes from Asian and Chinese grocers.

SPRING ROLLS

INGREDIENTS

Makes 26–30 rolls

FOR THE FILLING:
15 g/½ oz dried Chinese
  (shiitake) mushrooms
50 g/2 oz rice vermicelli
1–2 tbsp groundnut oil
1 small onion, peeled and
  finely chopped
3–4 garlic cloves, peeled and
  finely chopped
4 cm/1½ inch piece fresh root
  ginger, peeled and chopped
225 g/8 oz fresh pork mince
2 spring onions, trimmed and
  finely chopped
75 g/3 oz beansprouts

4 water chestnuts, chopped
2 tbsp freshly snipped chives
175 g/6 oz cooked peeled
  prawns, chopped
1 tsp oyster sauce
1 tsp soy sauce
salt and freshly ground black
  pepper
spring onion tassels, to garnish

FOR THE WRAPPERS:
4–5 tbsp plain flour
26–30 spring roll wrappers
300 ml/½ pint vegetable oil for
  deep frying

1 Soak the Chinese mushrooms in almost boiling water for 20 minutes. Remove and squeeze out the liquid. Discard any stems, slice and reserve. Soak the rice vermicelli as packet instructions.

2 Heat a large wok and when hot, add the oil. Heat then add the onion, garlic and ginger and stir-fry for 2 minutes.

3 Add the pork, spring onions and Chinese mushrooms and stir-fry for 4 minutes. Stir in the beansprouts, water chestnuts, chives, prawns, oyster and soy sauce. Season to taste with salt and pepper and spoon into a bowl.

4 Drain the noodles well, add to the bowl and toss until well mixed, then leave to cool.

5 Blend the flour to a smooth paste with 3–4 tablespoons of water. Soften a wrapper in a plate of warm water for 1–2 seconds, then drain. Put 2 tablespoons of the filling near one edge of the wrapper, fold the edge over the filling, then fold in each side and roll up. Seal with a little flour paste and transfer to a baking sheet, seam-side down. Repeat with the remaining wrappers.

6 Heat the oil in a large wok to 190°C/375°F, or until a cube of bread browns in 30 seconds. Fry the spring rolls a few at a time, until golden. Remove and drain on absorbent kitchen paper. Arrange on a serving plate and garnish with spring onion tassels. Serve immediately.

BARBECUE PORK STEAMED BUNS

INGREDIENTS   Serves 12

FOR THE BUNS:
175–200 g/6–7 oz plain flour
1 tbsp dried yeast
125 ml/4 fl oz milk
2 tbsp sunflower oil
1 tbsp sugar
½ tsp salt
spring onion tassels, to
   garnish
fresh green salad leaves,
   to serve

FOR THE FILLING:
2 tbsp vegetable oil
1 small red pepper, deseeded
   and finely chopped
2 garlic cloves, peeled and
   finely chopped
225 g/8 oz cooked pork, finely
   chopped
50 g/2 oz light brown sugar
50 ml/2 fl oz tomato ketchup
1–2 tsp hot chilli powder, or to
   taste

1 Put 75 g/3 oz of the flour in a bowl and stir in the yeast. Heat the milk, oil, sugar and salt in a small saucepan until warm, stirring until the sugar has dissolved. Pour into the bowl and, with an electric mixer, beat on a low speed for 30 seconds, scraping down the sides of the bowl, until blended. Beat at high speed for 3 minutes, then with a wooden spoon, stir in as much of the remaining flour as possible, until a stiff dough forms. Shape into a ball, place in a lightly oiled bowl, cover with clingfilm and leave for 1 hour in a warm place, or until doubled in size.

2 To make the filling, heat a wok, add the oil and when hot add the red pepper and garlic. Stir-fry for 4–5 minutes. Add the remaining ingredients and bring to the boil, stir-frying for 2–3 minutes until thick and syrupy. Cool and reserve.

3 Punch down the dough and turn onto a lightly floured surface. Divide into 12 pieces and shape them into balls, then cover and leave to rest for 5 minutes.

4 Roll each ball to a 7.5 cm/ 3 inch circle. Place a heaped tablespoon of filling in the centre of each. Dampen the edges, then bring them up and around the filling, pinching together to seal. Place seam-side down on a small square of non-stick baking parchment. Continue with the remaining dough and filling. Leave to rise for 10 minutes.

5 Bring a large wok half-filled with water to the boil, place the buns in a lightly oiled Chinese steamer, without touching each other. Cover and steam for 20–25 minutes, then remove and cool slightly. Garnish with spring onion tassels and serve with salad leaves.

CHICKEN-FILLED SPRING ROLLS

INGREDIENTS — Makes 12–14 rolls

FOR THE FILLING:
1 tbsp vegetable oil
2 slices streaky bacon, diced
225 g/8 oz skinless chicken breast fillets, thinly sliced
1 small red pepper, deseeded and finely chopped
4 spring onions, trimmed and finely chopped
2.5 cm/1 inch piece fresh root ginger, peeled and finely chopped
75 g/3 oz mangetout peas, thinly sliced

75 g/3 oz beansprouts
1 tbsp soy sauce
2 tsp Chinese rice wine or dry sherry
2 tsp hoisin or plum sauce

FOR THE WRAPPERS:
3 tbsp plain flour
12–14 spring roll wrappers
300 ml/½ pint vegetable oil for deep frying
shredded spring onions, to garnish
dipping sauce, to serve

1 Heat a large wok, add the oil and when hot add the diced bacon and stir-fry for 2–3 minutes, or until golden. Add the chicken and pepper and stir-fry for a further 2–3 minutes. Add the remaining filling ingredients and stir-fry 3–4 minutes until all the vegetables are tender. Turn into a colander and leave to drain as the mixture cools completely.

2 Blend the flour with about 1½ tablespoons of water to form a paste. Soften each wrapper in a plate of warm water for 1–2 seconds, then place on a chopping board. Put 2–3 tablespoons of filling on the near edge. Fold the edge over the filling to cover. Fold in each side and roll up. Seal the edge with a little flour paste and press to seal securely. Transfer to a baking sheet, seam-side down.

3 Heat the oil in a large wok to 190°C/375°F, or until a small cube of bread browns in about 30 seconds. Working in batches of 3–4, fry the spring rolls until they are crisp and golden, turning once (about 2 minutes). Remove and drain on absorbent kitchen paper. Arrange the spring rolls on a serving plate, garnish with spring onion tassels and serve hot with dipping sauce.

HELPFUL HINT

As always with wok cooking, it is important to cut all the ingredients into uniform small pieces. This will ensure that everything cooks quickly but will also make the spring rolls easier to roll.

FRIED PORK-FILLED WONTONS

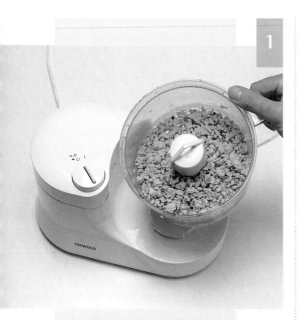

INGREDIENTS   Makes 24

FOR THE FILLING:

275 g/10 oz cooked pork, finely
    chopped

2–3 spring onions, trimmed
    and finely chopped

2.5 cm/1 inch piece fresh root
    ginger, grated

1 garlic clove, peeled and
    crushed

1 small egg, lightly beaten

1 tbsp soy sauce

1 tsp soft light brown sugar

1 tsp sweet chilli sauce or
    tomato ketchup

24–30 wonton wrappers,
    8 cm/3½ inches square

300 ml/½ pint vegetable oil for
    deep frying

**FOR THE GINGER DIPPING
    SAUCE:**

4 tbsp soy sauce

1–2 tbsp rice or raspberry
    vinegar

2.5 cm/1 inch piece fresh root
    ginger, peeled and finely
    slivered

1 tbsp sesame oil

1 tbsp soft light brown sugar

2–3 dashes hot chilli sauce

spring onion tassels, to
    garnish

1 Place all the filling ingredients into a food processor and, using the pulse button, process until well blended. Do not overwork, the filling should have a coarse texture.

2 Lay out the wonton wrappers on a clean chopping board and put a teaspoon of the filling in the centre of each.

3 Brush the edges with a little water and bring up 2 opposite corners of each square over the filling to form a triangle, pressing the edges firmly to seal. Dampen the 2 other corners and overlap them slightly, pressing firmly to seal, to form an oven-envelope shape, similar to a tortellini.

4 For the dipping sauce, stir together all the ingredients until the sugar is dissolved. Pour into a serving bowl and reserve.

5 Heat the oil in a large wok to 190°C/375°F, or until a small cube of bread browns in about 30 seconds.

6 Working in batches of 5–6, fry until the wontons are crisp and golden, turning once or twice. Remove and drain on absorbent kitchen paper. Garnish with spring onion tassels and serve hot with the dipping sauce.

PRAWN SALAD WITH TOASTED RICE

INGREDIENTS   Serves 4

FOR THE DRESSING:
50 ml/2 fl oz rice vinegar
1 red chilli, deseeded and
  thinly sliced
7.5 cm/3 inch piece lemon
  grass stalk, bruised
juice of 1 lime
2 tbsp Thai fish sauce
1 tsp sugar, or to taste

FOR THE SALAD:
350 g/12 oz large raw prawns,
  peeled with tails attached,
  heads removed

cayenne pepper
1 tbsp long-grain white rice
salt and freshly ground black
  pepper
2 tbsp sunflower oil
1 large head Chinese leaves or
  cos lettuce, shredded
½ small cucumber,
  peeled, deseeded and
  thinly sliced
1 small bunch chives, cut into
  2.5 cm/1 inch pieces
small bunch of mint leaves

1 Place all the ingredients for the dressing in a small bowl and leave to stand to let the flavours blend together.

2 Using a sharp knife, split each prawn lengthways in half, leaving the tail attached to one half. Remove any black vein and pat the prawns dry with absorbent kitchen paper. Sprinkle the prawns with a little salt and cayenne pepper and then reserve.

3 Heat a wok over a high heat. Add the rice and stir-fry until browned and fragrant. Turn into a mortar and cool. Crush gently with a pestle until coarse crumbs form. Wipe the wok clean.

4 Reheat the wok, add the oil and when hot, add the prawns and stir-fry for 2 minutes, or until pink. Transfer to a plate and season to taste with salt and pepper.

5 Place the Chinese leaves or lettuce into a salad bowl with the cucumber, chives and mint leaves and toss lightly together.

6 Remove the lemon grass stalk and some of the chilli from the dressing and pour all but 2 tablespoons over the salad and toss until lightly coated. Add the prawns and drizzle with the remaining dressing, then sprinkle with the toasted rice and serve.

STICKY BRAISED SPARE RIBS

INGREDIENTS

Serves 4

900 g/2 lb meaty pork spare ribs, cut crossways into 7.5 cm/3 inch pieces
125 ml/4 fl oz apricot nectar or orange juice
50 ml/2 fl oz dry white wine
3 tbsp black bean sauce
3 tbsp tomato ketchup
2 tbsp clear honey
3–4 spring onions, trimmed and chopped
2 garlic cloves, peeled and crushed

grated zest of 1 small orange
salt and freshly ground black pepper

TO GARNISH:
spring onion tassels
lemon wedges

1 Put the spare ribs in the wok and add enough cold water to cover. Bring to the boil over a medium-high heat, skimming any scum that rises to the surface. Cover and simmer for 30 minutes, then drain and rinse the ribs.

2 Rinse and dry the wok and return the ribs to it. In a bowl, blend the apricot nectar or orange juice with the white wine, black bean sauce, tomato ketchup and the honey until smooth.

3 Stir in the spring onions, garlic cloves and grated orange zest. Stir well until mixed thoroughly.

4 Pour the mixture over the spare ribs in the wok and stir gently until the ribs are lightly coated. Place over a moderate heat and bring to the boil.

5 Cover then simmer, stirring occasionally, for 1 hour, or until the ribs are tender and the sauce is thickened and sticky. (If the sauce reduces too quickly or begins to stick, add water 1 tablespoon at a time until the ribs are tender.) Adjust the seasoning to taste, then transfer the ribs to a serving plate and garnish with spring onion tassels and lemon wedges. Serve immediately.

HELPFUL HINT

It's probably best to get your butcher to cut the ribs into pieces for you, as they are quite bony. Boiling the ribs before cooking them in the sauce reduces the fat content and ensures that they are tender and more succulent.

SOY-GLAZED CHICKEN THIGHS

INGREDIENTS   Serves 6–8

900 g/2 lb chicken thighs
2 tbsp vegetable oil
3–4 garlic cloves, peeled and
 crushed
4 cm/1½ inch piece fresh root
 ginger, peeled and finely
 chopped or grated
125 ml/4 fl oz soy sauce

2–3 tbsp Chinese rice wine or
 dry sherry
2 tbsp clear honey
1 tbsp soft brown sugar
2–3 dashes hot chilli sauce, or
 to taste
freshly chopped parsley, to
 garnish

1 Heat a large wok and when hot add the oil and heat. Stir-fry the chicken thighs for 5 minutes or until golden. Remove and drain on absorbent kitchen paper. You may need to do this in 2–3 batches.

2 Pour off the oil and fat and, using absorbent kitchen paper, carefully wipe out the wok. Add the garlic, with the root ginger, soy sauce, Chinese rice wine or sherry and honey to the wok and stir well. Sprinkle in the soft brown sugar with the hot chilli sauce to taste, then place over the heat and bring to the boil.

3 Reduce the heat to a gentle simmer, then carefully add the chicken thighs. Cover the wok and simmer gently over a very low heat for 30 minutes, or until they are tender and the sauce is reduced and thickened and glazes the chicken thighs.

4 Stir or spoon the sauce occasionally over the chicken thighs and add a little water if the sauce is starting to become too thick. Arrange in a shallow serving dish, garnish with freshly chopped parsley and serve immediately.

TASTY TIP

Often overlooked, chicken wings are inexpensive and very flavourful. Served this way, with a sticky coating, they make an ideal snack. Serve with finger bowls.

SHREDDED DUCK IN LETTUCE LEAVES

INGREDIENTS

Serves 4–6

15 g/½ oz dried Chinese (shiitake) mushrooms

2 tbsp vegetable oil

400 g/14 oz boneless, skinless duck breast, cut crossways into thin strips

1 red chilli, deseeded and diagonally thinly sliced

4–6 spring onions, trimmed and diagonally sliced

2 garlic cloves, peeled and crushed

75 g/3 oz beansprouts

3 tbsp soy sauce

1 tbsp Chinese rice wine or dry sherry

1–2 tsp clear honey or brown sugar

4–6 tbsp hoisin sauce

large, crisp lettuce leaves such as iceberg or cos

handful of fresh mint leaves

dipping sauce (see Sesame Prawns, page 36)

1 Cover the dried Chinese mushrooms with almost boiling water, leave for 20 minutes, then drain and slice thinly.

2 Heat a large wok, add the oil and when hot stir-fry the duck for 3–4 minutes, or until sealed. Remove with a slotted spoon and reserve.

3 Add the chilli, spring onions, garlic and Chinese mushrooms to the wok and stir-fry for 2–3 minutes, or until softened.

4 Add the beansprouts, the soy sauce, Chinese rice wine or dry sherry and honey or brown sugar to the wok, and continue to stir-fry for 1 minute, or until blended.

5 Stir in the reserved duck and stir-fry for 2 minutes, or until well mixed together and heated right through. Transfer to a heated serving dish.

6 Arrange the hoisin sauce in a small bowl on a tray or plate with a pile of lettuce leaves and the mint leaves.

7 Let each guest spoon a little hoisin sauce onto a lettuce leaf, then top with a large spoonful of the stir-fried duck and vegetables and roll up the leaf to enclose the filling. Serve with the dipping sauce.

FOOD FACT

Hoisin sauce is a sweet and spicy aromatic Chinese sauce made primarily from soy beans, sugar, garlic and chilli.

SWEDISH COCKTAIL MEATBALLS

INGREDIENTS   Serves 4–6

50 g/2 oz butter
1 onion, peeled and finely
   chopped
50 g/2 oz fresh white
   breadcrumbs
1 medium egg, beaten
125 ml/4 fl oz double cream
salt and freshly ground black
   pepper

350 g/12 oz fresh lean
   beef mince
125 g/4 oz fresh pork mince
3–4 tbsp freshly chopped dill
½ tsp ground allspice
1 tbsp vegetable oil
125 ml/4 fl oz beef stock
cream cheese and chive or
   cranberry sauce, to serve

1 Heat half the butter in a large wok, add the onion and cook, stirring frequently, for 4–6 minutes, or until softened and beginning to colour. Transfer to a bowl and leave to cool. Wipe out the wok with absorbent kitchen paper.

2 Add the breadcrumbs and beaten egg with 1–2 tablespoons of cream to the softened onion. Season to taste with salt and pepper and stir until well blended. Using your fingertips crumble the beef and pork mince into the bowl.

3 Add half the dill, the allspice and, using your hands, mix together until well blended. With dampened hands, shape the mixture into 2.5 cm/ 1 inch balls.

4 Melt the remaining butter in the wok and add the vegetable oil, swirling it to coat the side of the wok.

5 Working in batches, add about one quarter to one third of the meatballs in a single layer and cook for 5 minutes, swirling and turning until golden and cooked.

6 Transfer to a plate and continue with the remaining meatballs, transferring them to the plate as they are cooked.

7 Pour off the fat in the wok. Add the beef stock and bring to the boil, then boil until reduced by half, stirring and scraping up any browned bits from the bottom. Add the remaining cream and continue to simmer until slightly thickened and reduced.

8 Stir in the remaining dill and season if necessary. Add the meatballs and simmer for 2–3 minutes, or until heated right through. Serve with cocktail sticks, with the sauce in a separate bowl for dipping.

FRESH TUNA SALAD

INGREDIENTS   Serves 4

225 g/8 oz mixed salad leaves
225 g/8 oz baby cherry
   tomatoes, halved
   lengthways
125 g/4 oz rocket leaves,
   washed
2 tbsp groundnut oil
550 g/1¼ lb boned tuna steaks,
   each cut into 4 small pieces

50 g/2 oz piece fresh
   Parmesan cheese

FOR THE DRESSING:
8 tbsp olive oil
grated zest and juice of
   2 small lemons
1 tbsp wholegrain mustard
salt and freshly ground
   black pepper

1 Wash the salad leaves and place in a large salad bowl with the cherry tomatoes and rocket and reserve.

2 Heat the wok, then add the oil and heat until almost smoking. Add the tuna, skin-side down, and cook for 4–6 minutes, turning once during cooking, or until cooked and the flesh flakes easily. Remove from the heat and leave to stand in the juices for 2 minutes before removing.

3 Meanwhile make the dressing, place the olive oil, lemon zest and juices and mustard in a small bowl or screw-topped jar and whisk or shake well until well blended. Season to taste with salt and pepper.

4 Transfer the tuna to a clean chopping board and flake, then add it to the salad and toss lightly.

5 Using a swivel blade vegetable peeler, peel the piece of Parmesan cheese into shavings. Divide the salad between 4 large serving plates, drizzle the dressing over the salad, then scatter with the Parmesan shavings.

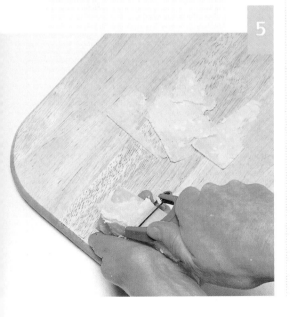

HELPFUL HINT

Bags of mixed salad leaves are available from all major supermarkets. Although they seem expensive, there is very little waste and they do save time. Rinse the leaves before using.

SALMON NOISETTES WITH FRUITY SAUCE

INGREDIENTS

Serves 4

4 x 125 g/4 oz salmon steaks
grated rind and juice of 2
    lemons
grated rind and juice of
    1 lime
3 tbsp olive oil
1 tbsp clear honey
1 tbsp wholegrain mustard
coarse sea salt and freshly
    ground black pepper
1 tbsp groundnut oil

125 g/4 oz mixed salad leaves,
    washed
1 bunch watercress, washed
    and thick stalks removed
250 g/9 oz baby plum
    tomatoes, halved

1 Using a sharp knife, cut the bone away from each salmon steak to create 2 salmon fillets. Repeat with the remaining salmon steaks. Shape the salmon fillets into noisettes and secure with fine string.

2 Mix together the citrus rinds and juices, olive oil, honey, wholegrain mustard, salt and pepper in a shallow dish. Add the salmon fillets and turn to coat. Cover and leave to marinate in the refrigerator for 4 hours, turning them occasionally in the marinade.

3 Heat the wok then add the groundnut oil and heat until hot. Lift out the salmon noisettes, reserving the marinade. Add the salmon to the wok and cook for 6–10 minutes, turning once during cooking, until

cooked and the fish is just flaking. Pour the marinade into the wok and heat through gently.

4 Mix together the salad leaves, watercress and tomatoes and arrange on serving plates. Top with the salmon noisettes and drizzle over any remaining warm marinade. Serve immediately.

HELPFUL HINT

When choosing salad leaves for this dish, look out for slightly bitter leaves such as frisée and radicchio, which will stand up well to the heat of the salmon and contrast well with the sweetness of the sauce.

SALMON WITH STRAWBERRY SAUCE

INGREDIENTS
Serves 4

4 x 150 g/5 oz salmon fillets
25 g/1 oz butter
2 tbsp groundnut oil
1 dessert apple, cored and cut into chunks
1 bunch spring onions, trimmed and diagonally sliced
1 garlic clove, peeled and sliced
50 g/2 oz pine nuts

juice of 1 lemon
125 g/4 oz strawberries, hulled and halved
1 bunch basil, freshly chopped
salt and freshly ground black pepper

TO SERVE:
freshly cooked creamy mashed potatoes
freshly cooked broad beans

1 Wash the salmon fillets and pat dry on absorbent kitchen paper. Heat the wok, then add the butter and half the oil and heat until bubbling. Cook the salmon fillets flesh side down for 5 minutes, until they are sealed. Then, using a fish slice, carefully turn the salmon fillets over and cook for a further 3–5 minutes, until the salmon flesh is just flaking.

2 Transfer the salmon fillets to warmed serving plates and keep warm in a low oven. Wipe the wok clean, then add the remaining oil to the wok and heat until almost smoking.

3 Add the apple chunks, spring onions, garlic slices and pine nuts and cook for 5 minutes, stirring occasionally, until they are golden brown.

4 Stir in the lemon juice, strawberries, chopped basil and season to taste with salt and pepper. Heat through thoroughly.

5 Spoon the sauce over the salmon fillets and serve immediately with creamy mashed potatoes and freshly cooked broad beans.

HELPFUL HINT

This unusual fruit sauce provides a much-needed sharpness against the richness of the fish. Do not overcook the strawberries, however, or they will lose their shape and texture.

STIR-FRIED TIGER PRAWNS

INGREDIENTS

Serves 4

75 g/3 oz fine egg thread
  noodles
125 g/4 oz broccoli florets
125 g/4 oz baby sweetcorn,
  halved
3 tbsp soy sauce
1 tbsp lemon juice
pinch of sugar
1 tsp chilli sauce
1 tsp sesame oil
2 tbsp sunflower oil
450 g/1 lb raw tiger prawns,
  peeled, heads and tails
  removed, and deveined

2.5 cm/1 inch piece fresh root
  ginger, peeled and cut into
  sticks
1 garlic clove, peeled and
  chopped
1 red chilli, deseeded and
  sliced
2 medium eggs, lightly beaten
227 g can water chestnuts,
  drained and sliced

1 Place the noodles in a large bowl, cover with plenty of boiling water and leave to stand for 5 minutes, or according to packet directions; stir occasionally. Drain and reserve. Blanch the broccoli and sweetcorn in a saucepan of boiling salted water for 2 minutes, then drain and reserve.

2 Meanwhile, mix together the soy sauce, lemon juice, sugar, chilli sauce and sesame oil in a bowl and reserve.

3 Heat a large wok, then add the sunflower oil and heat until just smoking. Add the prawns and stir-fry for 2–3 minutes, or until pink on all sides. Using a slotted spoon, transfer the prawns to a plate and reserve. Add the ginger and stir-fry for 30 seconds. Add the garlic

and chilli to the wok and cook for a further 30 seconds.

4 Add the noodles and stir-fry for 3 minutes, until the noodles are crisp. Stir in the prawns, vegetables, eggs and water chestnuts and stir-fry for a further 3 minutes, until the eggs are lightly cooked. Pour over the chilli sauce, stir lightly and serve immediately.

HELPFUL HINT

Egg noodles are available in a variety of thicknesses. All are very quick to cook and are an excellent store-cupboard ingredient.

CREAMY MIXED SEAFOOD WITH SPAGHETTI

INGREDIENTS   Serves 4

350 g/12 oz spaghetti
2 tbsp groundnut oil
1 bunch spring onions,
  trimmed and diagonally
  sliced
1 garlic clove, peeled and
  chopped
125 g/4 oz frozen peas
175 g/6 oz peeled prawns,
  thawed if frozen
¼ cucumber, peeled if
  preferred and chopped

150 ml/¼ pint dry vermouth or
  white wine
150 ml/¼ pint double cream
420 g can salmon, drained,
  boned, skinned and flaked
pinch of paprika
salt and freshly ground black
  pepper
50 g/2 oz freshly grated
  Parmesan cheese (optional)

1 Bring a large saucepan of salted water to the boil and add the spaghetti. Bring back to the boil and cook at a rolling boil for 8 minutes, or until 'al dente'. Drain thoroughly.

2 Meanwhile heat a large wok, then add the oil and heat until almost smoking. Stir-fry the spring onions for 2 minutes, then add the garlic and peas and stir-fry for 3 minutes.

3 Add the prawns and stir-fry for 2 minutes, until heated through and browned slightly. Add the cucumber and cook for 2 minutes.

4 Stir in the vermouth or white wine and bring to the boil. Simmer for 3 minutes, until reduced and thickened slightly.

Add the cream, stirring until well blended, then add the salmon and paprika. Bring almost to the boil, toss in the pasta and cook until heated through. Season to taste with salt and pepper, add the Parmesan cheese, if desired and serve immediately.

TASTY TIP

Choose canned red salmon for this recipe, rather than the cheaper pink salmon. The flavour is fuller and the texture is also better. If you don't like cleaning canned fish you can buy it skinned and boned.

COCONUT SEAFOOD

INGREDIENTS   Serves 4

2 tbsp groundnut oil

450 g/1 lb raw king prawns, peeled

2 bunches spring onions, trimmed and thickly sliced

1 garlic clove, peeled and chopped

2.5 cm/1 inch piece fresh root ginger, peeled and cut into matchsticks

125 g/4 oz fresh shiitake mushrooms, rinsed and halved

150 ml/¼ pint dry white wine

200 ml/7 fl oz carton coconut cream

4 tbsp freshly chopped coriander

salt and freshly ground black pepper

freshly cooked fragrant Thai rice

1 Heat a large wok, add the oil and heat until it is almost smoking, swirling the oil around the wok to coat the sides. Add the prawns and stir-fry over a high heat for 4-5 minutes, or until browned on all sides. Using a slotted spoon, transfer the prawns to a plate and keep warm in a low oven.

2 Add the spring onions, garlic and ginger to the wok and stir-fry for 1 minute. Add the mushrooms and stir-fry for a further 3 minutes. Using a slotted spoon, transfer the mushroom mixture to a plate and keep warm in a low oven.

3 Add the wine and coconut cream to the wok, bring to the boil and boil rapidly for 4 minutes, until reduced slightly.

4 Return the mushroom mixture and prawns to the wok, bring back to the boil, then simmer for 1 minute, stirring occasionally, until piping hot. Stir in the freshly chopped coriander and season to taste with salt and pepper. Serve immediately with the freshly cooked fragrant Thai rice.

HELPFUL HINT

If coconut cream is not available, grate 50 g/2 oz creamed coconut into 175 ml/6 fl oz hot water. Whisk until completely dissolved and use as above.

Lobster & Prawn Curry

INGREDIENTS

Serves 4

225 g/8 oz cooked lobster
meat, shelled if
necessary
225 g/8 oz raw tiger prawns,
peeled and deveined
2 tbsp groundnut oil
2 bunches spring onions,
trimmed and thickly
sliced
2 garlic cloves, peeled and
chopped
2.5 cm/1 inch piece fresh root
ginger, peeled and cut into
matchsticks

2 tbsp Thai red curry paste
grated zest and juice of 1 lime
200 ml/7 fl oz coconut cream
salt and freshly ground black
pepper
3 tbsp freshly chopped
coriander
freshly cooked Thai fragrant
rice, to serve

1 Using a sharp knife, slice the lobster meat thickly. Wash the tiger prawns and pat dry with absorbent kitchen paper. Make a small 1 cm/½ inch cut at the tail end of each prawn and reserve.

2 Heat a large wok, then add the oil and, when hot, stir-fry the lobster and tiger prawns for 4–6 minutes, or until pink. Using a slotted spoon, transfer to a plate and keep warm in a low oven.

3 Add the spring onions and stir-fry for 2 minutes, then stir in the garlic and ginger and stir-fry for a further 2 minutes. Add the curry paste and stir-fry for 1 minute.

4 Pour in the coconut cream, lime zest and juice and the seasoning. Bring to the boil and simmer for 1 minute. Return the prawns and lobster and any juices to the wok and simmer for 2 minutes. Stir in two-thirds of the freshly chopped coriander to the wok mixture, then sprinkle with the remaining coriander and serve immediately.

FOOD FACT

This dish is not as expensive as it first appears, since 1 small lobster is easily enough for 4 people.

SMOKED SALMON WITH BROAD BEANS & RICE

INGREDIENTS   Serves 4

2 tbsp sunflower oil
25 g/1 oz unsalted butter
1 onion, peeled and chopped
2 garlic cloves, peeled and
  chopped
175 g/6 oz asparagus tips,
  halved
75 g/3 oz frozen broad beans
150 ml/¼ pint dry white wine
125 g/4 oz sun-dried tomatoes,
  drained and sliced

125 g/4 oz baby spinach
  leaves, washed
450 g/1 lb cooked long-grain
  rice
3 tbsp crème fraîche
225 g/8 oz smoked salmon, cut
  into strips
75 g/3 oz freshly grated
  Parmesan cheese
salt and freshly ground black
  pepper

1 Heat a large wok, then add the oil and butter and, when melted, stir-fry the onion for 3 minutes, until almost softened. Add the garlic and asparagus tips and stir-fry for 3 minutes. Add the broad beans and wine and bring to the boil, then simmer, stirring occasionally, until the wine is reduced slightly.

2 Add the sun-dried tomatoes and bring back to the boil, then simmer for 2 minutes. Stir in the baby spinach leaves and cooked rice and return to the boil. Stir-fry for 2 minutes, or until the spinach is wilted and the rice is heated through thoroughly.

3 Stir in the crème fraîche, smoked salmon strips and Parmesan cheese. Stir well and cook, stirring frequently, until piping hot. Season to taste with salt and pepper. Serve immediately.

HELPFUL HINT

To make 450 g/1 lb cooked rice, measure 175 g/6 oz long-grain rice. Wash well in several changes of water and drain. Put into a saucepan with enough cold water to cover the rice by about 2.5 cm/ 1 inch, add salt and stir well. Bring to the boil over a high heat, then reduce the heat to very low, cover and cook for 10 minutes. Remove from the heat and leave, covered, for a further 10 minutes. Do not lift the lid until the full 20 minutes have elapsed.

SPECIAL FRIED RICE

INGREDIENTS   Serves 4

knob of butter
4 medium eggs, beaten
4 tbsp groundnut oil
1 bunch spring onions,
   trimmed and finely shredded
125 g/4 oz cooked ham, diced
350 g/12 oz large cooked
   prawns, thawed if frozen and
   peeled
125 g/4 oz peas, thawed if
   frozen

450 g/1 lb cooked long-grain
   rice
2 tbsp dark soy sauce
1 tbsp sherry
salt and freshly ground black
   pepper
1 tbsp freshly shredded
   coriander

1 Heat a wok, lightly grease with the butter and when melted, pour in half the beaten eggs. Cook for 4 minutes, stirring frequently, until the egg has set, forming an omelette. Using a fish slice, lift the omelette from the wok and roll up into a sausage shape. When cool, using a sharp knife, slice the omelette into thin rings, then reserve.

2 Wipe the wok clean with absorbent kitchen paper and heat it. Add the oil and heat until just smoking. Add the shredded spring onions, the ham, prawns and peas and stir-fry for 2 minutes, or until heated through thoroughly. Add the cooked rice and stir-fry for a further 2 minutes.

3 Stir in the remaining beaten eggs and stir-fry for 3 minutes, or until the egg has set. Stir in the soy sauce and sherry and season to taste with salt and

pepper, then heat until piping hot. Add the omelette rings and gently stir through the mixture, making sure not to break up the omelette rings. Sprinkle with the freshly shredded coriander and serve immediately.

HELPFUL HINT

Use cold cooked rice
(see Helpful Hint in previous
recipe for cooking) as it is
less likely to stick to the wok.
Make sure, however, that the
rice is heated right through
and is piping hot. Do not
re-heat more than once
and never keep cooked rice
longer than 24 hours.

CHILLI MONKFISH STIR FRY

INGREDIENTS   Serves 4

350 g/12 oz pasta twists	**FOR THE MARINADE:**
550 g/1¼ lb monkfish, trimmed	1 garlic clove, peeled and
and cut into chunks	chopped
2 tbsp groundnut oil	2 tbsp dark soy sauce
1 green chilli, deseeded	grated zest and juice of
and cut into matchsticks	1 lime
2 tbsp sesame seeds	1 tbsp sweet chilli sauce
pinch of cayenne pepper	4 tbsp olive oil
sliced green chillies, to	
garnish	

1 Bring a large saucepan of lightly salted water to the boil and add the pasta. Stir, bring back to the boil and cook at a rolling boil for 8 minutes, or until 'al dente'. Drain thoroughly and reserve.

2 For the marinade, mix together the sliced garlic, dark soy sauce, lime zest and juice, sweet chilli sauce and olive oil in a shallow dish, then add the monkfish chunks. Stir until all the monkfish is lightly coated in the marinade, then cover and leave in the refrigerator for at least 30 minutes, spooning the marinade over the fish occasionally.

3 Heat a wok, then add the oil and heat until almost smoking. Remove the monkfish from the marinade, scraping off as much marinade as possible, add to the wok and stir-fry for 3 minutes. Add the green chilli and sesame seeds and stir-fry the mixture for a further 1 minute.

4 Stir in the pasta and marinade and stir-fry for 1–2 minutes, or until piping hot. Sprinkle with cayenne pepper and garnish with sliced green chillies. Serve immediately.

HELPFUL HINT

Although a fishmonger will bone the monkfish, it is very simple to do. Clean the fish of any skin or membrane. With a large sharp knife, feel for the bone that runs down the centre of the fish. Keeping the knife as close to the bone as possible, cut down the length of the fish on either side of the bone to remove the fillets.

TERIYAKI SALMON

INGREDIENTS   Serves 4

450 g/1 lb salmon fillet, skinned
6 tbsp Japanese teriyaki sauce
1 tbsp rice wine vinegar
1 tbsp tomato paste
dash of Tabasco sauce
grated zest of ½ lemon
salt and freshly ground black
  pepper

4 tbsp groundnut oil
1 carrot, peeled and cut into
  matchsticks
125 g/4 oz mangetout peas
125 g/4 oz oyster mushrooms,
  wiped

1 Using a sharp knife, cut the salmon into thick slices and place in a shallow dish. Mix together the teriyaki sauce, rice wine vinegar, tomato paste, Tabasco sauce, lemon zest and seasoning. Spoon the marinade over the salmon, then cover loosely and leave to marinate in the refrigerator for 30 minutes, turning the salmon or spooning the marinade occasionally over the salmon.

2 Heat a large wok, then add 2 tablespoons of the oil until almost smoking. Stir-fry the carrot for 2 minutes, then add the mangetout peas and stir-fry for a further 2 minutes. Add the oyster mushrooms and stir-fry for 4 minutes, until softened. Using a slotted spoon, transfer the vegetables to 4 warmed serving plates and keep warm.

3 Remove the salmon from the marinade, reserving both the salmon and marinade. Add the remaining oil to the wok, heat until almost smoking, then cook the salmon for 4–5 minutes, turning once during cooking, or until the fish is just flaking. Add the marinade and heat through for 1 minute. Serve immediately, with the salmon arranged on top of the vegetables and the marinade drizzled over.

TASTY TIP

Teriyaki sauce is available ready-made, but to make your own, mix together 2 tablespoons sake, 2 tablespoons mirin, 2 tablespoons Japanese soy sauce (such as Kikkoman) and 2 tablespoons sugar. Whisk together until the sugar has dissolved and use as above.

GOUJONS OF PLAICE WITH TARTARE SAUCE

INGREDIENTS   Serves 4

75 g/3 oz fresh white
  breadcrumbs
3 tbsp freshly grated
  Parmesan cheese
salt and freshly ground black
  pepper
1 tbsp dried oregano
1 medium egg
450 g/1 lb plaice fillets
300 ml/½ pint vegetable oil for
  deep frying
fat chips, to serve

FOR THE TARTARE SAUCE:
200 ml/7 fl oz prepared
  mayonnaise
50 g/2 oz gherkins, finely
  chopped
2 tbsp freshly snipped chives
1 garlic clove, peeled and
  crushed
2–3 tbsp capers, drained and
  chopped
pinch of cayenne pepper
sunflower oil for deep frying

1 Mix together the breadcrumbs, Parmesan cheese, seasoning and oregano on a large plate. Lightly beat the egg in a shallow dish. Then, using a sharp knife, cut the plaice fillets into thick strips. Coat the plaice strips in the beaten egg, allowing any excess to drip back into the dish, then dip the strips into the breadcrumbs until well coated. Place the goujons on a baking sheet, cover and chill in the refrigerator for 30 minutes.

2 Meanwhile, to make the tartare sauce, mix together the mayonnaise, gherkins, chives, garlic, capers and cayenne pepper. Stir, then season to taste with salt and pepper. Place in a bowl, cover loosely and store in the refrigerator until required.

3 Pour the oil into a large wok. Heat to 190°C/375°F, or until a small cube of bread turns golden and crisp in about 30 seconds. Cook the plaice goujons in batches for about 4 minutes, turning occasionally, until golden. Using a slotted spoon, remove and drain on absorbent kitchen paper. Serve immediately with the tartare sauce and chips.

TASTY TIP

For a change, try replacing the white bread in this recipe with flavoured foccacia or ciabatta.

ORIENTAL SPICY SCALLOPS

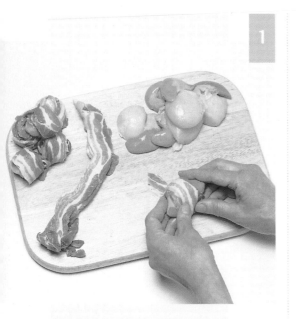

INGREDIENTS   Serves 6

12 fresh scallops, trimmed

12 rashers smoked streaky
bacon, derinded

2 tbsp groundnut oil

1 red onion, peeled and cut
into wedges

1 red pepper, deseeded and
sliced

1 yellow pepper, deseeded
and sliced

2 garlic cloves, peeled and
chopped

½ tsp garam masala

1 tbsp tomato paste

1 tbsp paprika

4 tbsp freshly chopped
coriander

TO SERVE:

freshly cooked noodles

Oriental-style salad

1 Remove the thin black thread from the scallops, rinse lightly and pat dry on absorbent kitchen paper. Wrap each scallop in a bacon rasher. Place on a baking sheet, cover and chill in the refrigerator for 30 minutes.

2 Meanwhile heat the wok, then add 1 tablespoon of the oil and stir-fry the onion for 3 minutes, or until almost softened. Add the peppers and stir-fry for 5 minutes, stirring occasionally, until browned. Using a slotted spoon, transfer the vegetables to a plate and reserve.

3 Add the remaining oil to the wok, heat until almost smoking and then add the scallops, seam-side down, and stir-fry for 2–3 minutes. Turn the scallops over and stir-fry for a further 2–3 minutes, until the bacon is crisp and the scallops are almost tender.

Add the garlic, garam masala, tomato paste and paprika and stir until the scallops are lightly coated.

4 Stir in the remaining ingredients with the reserved vegetables. Stir-fry for a further 1–2 minutes or until the vegetables are piping hot. Serve immediately with noodles and an Oriental salad.

HELPFUL HINT

If you buy live scallops, to remove them from the shell, hold the flat part of the shell in your palm and slice a sharp knife between the shell halves, keeping the blade flat against the bottom shell. Slice through the meat, away from your hand, and open the shell. Cut the meat from the rounded shell. Remove the grey 'frill' and wash well.

CRISPY PRAWN STIR FRY

INGREDIENTS   Serves 4

3 tbsp soy sauce
1 tsp cornflour
pinch of sugar
6 tbsp groundnut oil
450 g/1 lb raw shelled tiger
  prawns, halved lengthways
125 g/4 oz carrots, peeled and
  cut into matchsticks
2.5 cm/1 inch piece fresh root
  ginger, peeled and cut into
  matchsticks

125 g/4 oz mangetout peas,
  trimmed and shredded
125 g/4 oz asparagus spears,
  cut into short lengths
125 g/4 oz beansprouts
¼ head Chinese leaves,
  shredded
2 tsp sesame oil

1 Mix together the soy sauce, cornflour and sugar in a small bowl and reserve.

2 Heat a large wok, then add 3 tablespoons of the oil and heat until almost smoking. Add the prawns and stir-fry for 4 minutes, or until pink all over. Using a slotted spoon, transfer the prawns to a plate and keep warm in a low oven.

3 Add the remaining oil to the wok and when just smoking, add the carrots and ginger and stir-fry for 1 minute, or until slightly softened, then add the mangetout peas and stir-fry for a further 1 minute. Add the asparagus and stir-fry for 4 minutes, or until softened.

4 Add the beansprouts and Chinese leaves and stir-fry for 2 minutes, or until the leaves are slightly wilted. Pour in the soy sauce mixture and return the prawns to the wok. Stir-fry over a medium heat until piping hot, then add the sesame oil, give a final stir and serve immediately.

HELPFUL HINT

The long list of ingredients need not be daunting. As always with wok cooking, good preparation saves a lot of time. It is essential to cut everything into small, uniform pieces and have everything ready before starting to cook.

SPICY COD RICE

INGREDIENTS   Serves 4

1 tbsp plain flour
1 tbsp freshly chopped
  coriander
1 tsp ground cumin
1 tsp ground coriander
550 g/1¼ lb thick-cut cod fillet,
  skinned and cut into large
  chunks
4 tbsp groundnut oil
50 g/2 oz cashew nuts
1 bunch spring onions,
  trimmed and diagonally
  sliced

1 red chilli, deseeded and
  chopped
1 carrot, peeled and cut into
  matchsticks
125 g/4 oz frozen peas
450 g/1 lb cooked long-grain
  rice
2 tbsp sweet chilli sauce
2 tbsp soy sauce

1 Mix together the flour, coriander, cumin and ground coriander on a large plate. Coat the cod in the spice mixture then place on a baking sheet, cover and chill in the refrigerator for 30 minutes.

2 Heat a large wok, then add 2 tablespoons of the oil and heat until almost smoking. Stir-fry the cashew nuts for 1 minute, until browned, then remove and reserve.

3 Add a further 1 tablespoon of the oil and heat until almost smoking. Add the cod and stir-fry for 2 minutes. Using a fish slice, turn the cod pieces over and cook for a further 2 minutes, until golden. Remove from the wok, place on a warm plate, cover and keep warm.

4 Add the remaining oil to the wok, heat until almost smoking then stir-fry the spring onions and chilli for 1 minute before adding the carrots and peas and stir-frying for a further 2 minutes. Stir in the rice, chilli sauce, soy sauce and cashew nuts and stir-fry for 3 more minutes. Add the cod, heat for 1 minute, then serve immediately.

HELPFUL HINT

Care is needed when frying nuts as they have a tendency to turn from golden to burnt very quickly. An alternative is to toast them on a baking sheet in the oven at 180°C/350°F/Gas Mark 4 for about 5 minutes until they are golden and fragrant.

SOLE WITH RED WINE SAUCE

INGREDIENTS   Serves 4

4 tbsp groundnut oil

125 g/4 oz rindless smoked streaky bacon, diced

175 g/6 oz shallots, peeled and chopped

225 g/8 oz button mushrooms, wiped

1 tbsp plain flour

2 tbsp brandy

300 ml/½ pint red wine

1 bouquet garni

1 garlic clove, peeled and chopped

salt and freshly ground black pepper

8 sole fillets, skinned and cut in half

sprigs of fresh parsley, to garnish

TO SERVE:

freshly cooked noodles

mangetout peas

1 Heat a large wok, add the oil and heat. When almost smoking, stir-fry the bacon and shallots for 4–5 minutes, or until golden. Using a slotted spoon remove from the wok and keep warm. Add the mushrooms and stir-fry for 2 minutes, then remove and reserve.

2 Sprinkle the flour into the wok and carefully stir-fry over a medium heat for 30 seconds. Remove the wok from the heat, then return the bacon and shallots to the wok together with the brandy.

3 Stir in the red wine, bouquet garni, garlic and season to taste with salt and pepper. Return to the heat and bring back to the boil, stirring until smooth, then simmer for about 5 minutes, until the sauce is thickened.

4 Meanwhile, roll the sole fillets up and secure with either fine twine or cocktail sticks. Carefully add the rolled-up sole fillets and reserved mushrooms with seasoning to the wok. Reduce the heat, cover with a lid or tinfoil and simmer for a further 8–10 minutes, or until the fish is tender. Discard the bouquet garni, garnish with sprigs of fresh parsley and serve immediately with freshly cooked noodles and steamed mangetout peas.

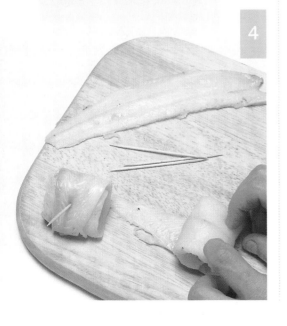

HELPFUL HINT

Either lemon sole or Dover sole may be used in this recipe, depending on the budget.

TROUT WITH CREAM SAUCE

INGREDIENTS   Serves 4

550 g/1¼ lb rainbow
   trout fillets, cut into
   pieces
salt and freshly ground
   black pepper
2 tbsp plain white flour
1 tbsp finely chopped dill
groundnut oil for frying

FOR THE CREAM SAUCE:
50 g/2 oz butter
2 bunches spring onions,
   trimmed and thickly sliced

1 garlic clove, peeled and
   finely chopped
300 ml/½ pint dry white wine
150 ml/¼ pint double cream
3 tomatoes, skinned,
   deseeded and cut into
   wedges
3 tbsp freshly chopped basil
freshly snipped basil, to
   garnish
freshly cooked creamed herb
   potatoes, to serve

1 Remove as many of the tiny pin bones as possible from the trout fillets, rinse lightly and pat dry on absorbent kitchen paper. Season the flour and stir in the chopped dill, then use to coat the trout fillets.

2 Pour sufficient oil into a large wok to a depth of 2.5 cm/1 inch deep. Heat until hot and cook the trout in batches for about 3–4 minutes, turning occasionally, or until cooked. Using a slotted spoon, remove and drain on absorbent kitchen paper and keep warm. You may need to cook the trout in batches. Drain the wok and wipe clean.

3 Melt 25 g/1 oz of the butter in the wok, then stir-fry the spring onions and garlic for 2 minutes. Add the wine, bring to the boil and boil rapidly until reduced by half. Stir in the cream,

with the tomatoes and basil, and bring to the boil. Simmer for 1 minute, then add seasoning to taste.

4 Add the trout to the sauce and heat through until piping hot. Garnish with freshly snipped basil and serve immediately on a bed of creamed herb potatoes.

HELPFUL HINT

Before cutting into pieces, lay the trout fillets on a clean chopping board and run your fingers from the tail end of the fish up to the head end. Use a pair of tweezers to remove any fine (pin) bones that you can feel.

CREAMY SPICY SHELLFISH

INGREDIENTS   Serves 4

2 tbsp groundnut oil

1 onion, peeled and chopped

2.5 cm/1 inch piece fresh root
   ginger, peeled and grated

225 g/8 oz queen scallops,
   cleaned and rinsed

1 garlic clove, peeled and
   chopped

2 tsp ground cumin

1 tsp paprika

1 tsp coriander seeds, crushed

3 tbsp lemon juice

2 tbsp sherry

300 ml/½ pint fish stock

150 ml/¼ pint double cream

225 g/8 oz peeled prawns

225 g/8 oz cooked mussels,
   shelled

salt and freshly ground black
   pepper

2 tbsp freshly chopped
   coriander

1 Heat a large wok, then add the oil and when hot, stir-fry the onion and ginger for 2 minutes, or until softened. Add the scallops and stir-fry for 2 minutes, or until the scallops are just cooked. Using a slotted spoon, carefully transfer the scallops to a bowl and keep warm in a low oven.

2 Stir in the garlic, ground cumin, paprika and crushed coriander seeds and cook for 1 minute, stirring constantly. Pour in the lemon juice, sherry and fish stock and bring to the boil. Boil rapidly until reduced by half and slightly thickened.

3 Stir in the cream and return the scallops and any scallop juices to the wok. Bring to the boil and simmer for 1 minute. Add the prawns and mussels and heat through until piping hot. Season to taste with salt and

pepper. Sprinkle with freshly chopped coriander and serve immediately.

HELPFUL HINT

Queen scallops are difficult to find on the shell. They are usually bought frozen, therefore tend to have a lot of water in them. They should be drained well and pressed carefully between sheets of absorbent kitchen paper to remove the excess moisture, which will help to keep them from shrinking.

SQUID & PRAWNS WITH SAFFRON RICE

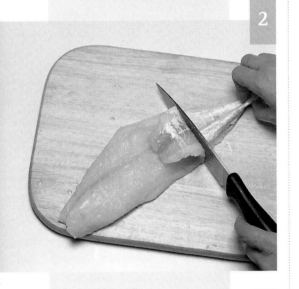

INGREDIENTS   Serves 4

2 tbsp groundnut oil

1 large onion, peeled and sliced

2 garlic cloves, peeled and chopped

450 g/1 lb tomatoes, skinned, deseeded and chopped

225 g/8 oz long-grain rice

¼ tsp saffron strands

600 ml/1 pint fish stock

225 g/8 oz firm fish fillets, such as monkfish or cod

225 g/8 oz squid, cleaned

225 g/8 oz mussels with shells

75 g/3 oz frozen or shelled fresh peas

225 g/8 oz peeled prawns, thawed if frozen

salt and freshly ground black pepper

TO GARNISH:

8 whole cooked prawns

lemon wedges

1 Heat a large wok, add the oil and when hot, stir-fry the onion and garlic for 3 minutes. Add the tomatoes and continue to stir-fry for 1 minute before adding the rice, saffron and stock. Bring to the boil, reduce the heat, cover and simmer for 10 minutes, stirring occasionally.

2 Meanwhile, remove any skin from the fish fillets, rinse lightly and cut into small cubes. Rinse the squid, pat dry with absorbent kitchen paper, then cut into rings and reserve. Scrub the mussels, discarding any that stay open after being tapped on the work surface. Cover with cold water and reserve until required.

3 Add the peas to the wok together with the fish and return to a gentle simmer. Cover and simmer for 5–10 minutes, or until the rice is tender and most of the liquid has been absorbed.

4 Uncover and stir in the squid, the drained prepared mussels and the peeled prawns. Re-cover and simmer for 5 minutes, or until the mussels have opened. Discard any unopened ones. Season to taste with salt and pepper. Garnish with whole cooked prawns and lemon wedges, then serve immediately.

HELPFUL HINT

Skin tomatoes by making a cross on the top of each one, cover with boiling water, the leave for 2 minutes. Drain and peel.

TEMPURA

INGREDIENTS   Serves 4

FOR THE BATTER:
200 g/7 oz plain flour
pinch of bicarbonate of soda
1 medium egg yolk

FOR THE PRAWNS & VEGETABLES:
8–12 raw king size prawns
1 carrot, peeled
125 g/4 oz button mushrooms, wiped

1 green pepper, deseeded
1 small aubergine, trimmed
1 onion, peeled
125 g/4 oz French beans
125 ml/4 fl oz sesame oil
300 ml/½ pint vegetable oil for deep frying

TO SERVE:
soy sauce
chilli dipping sauce

1 Sift the flour and bicarbonate of soda into a mixing bowl. Blend 450 ml/¾ pint water and the egg yolk together, then gradually whisk into the flour mixture until a smooth batter is formed.

2 Peel the prawns, leaving the tails intact, de-vein, then rinse lightly and pat dry with absorbent kitchen paper and reserve. Slice the carrot thinly then, using small pastry cutters, cut out fancy shapes. Cut the mushrooms in half, if large, and cut the pepper into chunks. Slice the aubergine, then cut into chunks, together with the onion, and finally trim the French beans.

3 Pour the sesame oil and the vegetable oil into a large wok and heat to 180°C/350°F, or until a small spoonful of the batter dropped into the oil sizzles and cooks on impact.

4 Dip the prawns and vegetables into the reserved batter (no more than 8 pieces at a time) and stir until lightly coated. Cook for 3 minutes, turning occasionally during cooking, or until evenly golden. Using a slotted spoon, transfer the prawns and vegetables onto absorbent kitchen paper and drain well. Keep warm. Repeat with the remaining ingredients. Serve immediately with soy sauce and chilli dipping sauce.

FOOD FACT

The bicarbonate of soda in the batter helps it to rise quickly when it hits the hot oil and then helps to keep the batter crisp once it is drained.

MEATBALLS WITH BEAN & TOMATO SAUCE

INGREDIENTS

Serves 4

1 large onion, peeled and
finely chopped

1 red pepper, deseeded and
chopped

1 tbsp freshly chopped oregano

½ tsp hot paprika

425 g can red kidney beans,
drained

300 g/11 oz fresh beef mince

salt and freshly ground black
pepper

4 tbsp sunflower oil

1 garlic clove, peeled and
crushed

400 g can chopped
tomatoes

1 tbsp freshly chopped
coriander, to garnish

freshly cooked rice, to serve

1 Make the meatballs by blending half the onion, half the red pepper, the oregano, the paprika and 350 g/12 oz of the kidney beans in a blender or food processor for a few seconds. Add the beef with seasoning and blend until well mixed. Turn the mixture onto a lightly floured board and form into small balls.

2 Heat the wok, then add 2 tablespoons of the oil and, when hot, stir-fry the meatballs gently until well browned on all sides. Remove with a slotted spoon and keep warm.

3 Wipe the wok clean, then add the remaining oil and cook the remaining onion and pepper and the garlic for 3–4 minutes, until soft. Add the tomatoes, seasoning to taste and remaining kidney beans.

4 Return the meatballs to the wok, stir them into the sauce, then cover and simmer for 10 minutes. Sprinkle with the chopped coriander and serve immediately with the freshly cooked rice.

FOOD FACT

Paprika gives this dish its distinctive flavour and colour. Made from dried peppers, it is available hot or mild and even smoked. The best paprika comes from either Hungary or Spain, where in both places it is widely used.

CRISPY PORK WITH TANGY SAUCE

INGREDIENTS
Serves 4

350 g/12 oz pork fillet
1 tbsp light soy sauce
1 tbsp dry sherry
salt and freshly ground black
  pepper
1 tbsp sherry vinegar
1 tbsp tomato paste
1 tbsp dark soy sauce
2 tsp light muscovado sugar
150 ml/¼ pint chicken stock
1½ tsp clear honey

8 tsp cornflour
450 ml/¾ pint groundnut oil
  for frying
1 medium egg

TO GARNISH:
fresh sprigs of dill
orange wedges

1 Remove and discard any fat and sinew from the pork fillet, then cut into 2 cm/¾ inch cubes and place in a shallow dish. Blend the light soy sauce with the dry sherry and add seasoning. Pour over the pork and stir until the pork is lightly coated. Cover and leave to marinate in the refrigerator for at least 30 minutes, stirring occasionally.

2 Meanwhile, blend the sherry vinegar, tomato paste, dark soy sauce, light muscovado sugar, chicken stock and honey together in a small saucepan and heat gently, stirring occasionally, until the sugar has dissolved. Then bring to the boil.

3 Blend 2 teaspoons of cornflour with 1 tablespoon of water and stir into the sauce. Cook, stirring, until smooth and thickened, and either keep warm or reheat when required.

4 Heat the oil in the wok to 190°C/375°F. Whisk together the remaining 6 teaspoons of cornflour and the egg to make a smooth batter. Drain the pork if necessary, then dip the pieces into the batter, allowing any excess to drip back into the bowl. Cook in the hot oil for 2–3 minutes, or until golden and tender. Drain on kitchen paper. Cook the pork in batches until it is all cooked, then garnish and serve immediately with the sauce.

HELPFUL HINT

Mix cornflour with a little of the hot, not boiling, sauce or blend to a paste with a little cold liquid. Stir into the hot liquor and cook stirring to thicken.

BEEF FAJITAS WITH AVOCADO SAUCE

INGREDIENTS

Serves 3–6

2 tbsp sunflower oil
450 g/1 lb beef fillet or rump steak, trimmed and cut into thin strips
2 garlic cloves, peeled and crushed
1 tsp ground cumin
¼ tsp cayenne pepper
1 tbsp paprika
230 g can chopped tomatoes
215 g can red kidney beans, drained

1 tbsp freshly chopped coriander
1 avocado, peeled, pitted and chopped
1 shallot, peeled and chopped
1 large tomato, skinned, deseeded and chopped
1 red chilli, diced
1 tbsp lemon juice
6 large flour tortilla pancakes
3–4 tbsp soured cream
green salad, to serve

1 Heat the wok, add the oil, then stir-fry the beef for 3–4 minutes. Add the garlic and spices and continue to cook for a further 2 minutes. Stir the tomatoes into the wok, bring to the boil, cover and simmer gently for 5 minutes.

2 Meanwhile, blend the kidney beans in a food processor until slightly broken up, then add to the wok. Continue to cook for a further 5 minutes, adding 2–3 tablespoons of water. The mixture should be thick and fairly dry. Stir in the chopped coriander.

3 Mix the chopped avocado, shallot, tomato, chilli and lemon juice together. Spoon into a serving dish and reserve.

4 When ready to serve, warm the tortillas and spread with a little soured cream. Place a spoonful of the beef mixture on top, followed by a spoonful of the avocado sauce, then roll up. Repeat until all the mixture is used up. Serve immediately with a green salad.

HELPFUL HINT

The avocado sauce should not be made too far in advance, as avocado has a tendency to discolour. If it is necessary to make it some time ahead, the surface of the sauce should be covered with clingfilm.

CARIBBEAN PORK

INGREDIENTS
Serves 4

450 g/1 lb pork fillet
2.5 cm/1 inch piece fresh root
  ginger, peeled and grated
½ tsp crushed dried chillies
2 garlic cloves, peeled and
  crushed
2 tbsp freshly chopped parsley
150 ml/¼ pint orange juice
2 tbsp dark soy sauce
2 tbsp groundnut oil

1 large onion, peeled and
  sliced into wedges
1 large courgette (about
  225 g/8 oz), trimmed and
  cut into strips
1 orange pepper, deseeded
  and cut into strips
1 ripe but firm mango, peeled
  and pitted
freshly cooked rice to serve

1 Cut the pork fillet into thin strips and place in a shallow dish. Sprinkle with the ginger, chillies, garlic and 1 tablespoon of the parsley. Blend together the orange juice, soy sauce and 1 tablespoon of the oil, then pour over the pork. Cover and chill in the refrigerator for 30 minutes, stirring occasionally. Remove the pork strips with a slotted spoon and reserve the marinade.

2 Heat the wok, pour in the remaining oil and stir-fry the pork for 3–4 minutes. Add the onion rings and the courgette and pepper strips and cook for 2 minutes. Add the reserved marinade to the wok and stir-fry for a further 2 minutes.

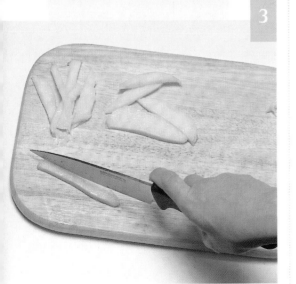

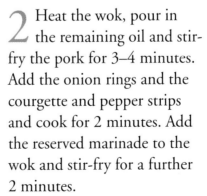

3 Remove the stone from the mango, cut the flesh into strips, then stir it into the pork mixture. Continue to stir-fry

until everything is piping hot. Garnish with the remaining parsley and serve immediately with plenty of freshly cooked rice.

HELPFUL HINT

Pork fillet, or tenderloin, as it is sometimes known, is a very tender cut and is always boneless. It may have some sinew attached and this should be removed with a sharp knife.

SAUSAGE & BACON RISOTTO

INGREDIENTS   Serves 4

225 g/8 oz long-grain rice
1 tbsp olive oil
25 g/1 oz butter
175 g/6 oz cocktail sausages
1 shallot, peeled and finely
  chopped
75 g/3 oz bacon lardons or
  thick slices of streaky bacon,
  chopped
150 g/5 oz chorizo or similar
  spicy sausage, cut into chunks

1 green pepper, deseeded and
  cut into strips
197 g can sweetcorn,
  drained
2 tbsp freshly chopped parsley
50 g/2 oz mozzarella cheese,
  grated

1 Cook the rice in a saucepan of boiling salted water for 15 minutes or until tender, or according to packet instructions. Drain and rinse in cold water. Drain again and leave until completely cold.

2 Meanwhile, heat the wok, pour in the oil and melt the butter. Cook the cocktail sausages, turning continuously until cooked. Remove with a slotted spoon, cut in half and keep warm.

3 Add the chopped shallot and bacon to the wok and cook for 2–3 minutes until cooked but not browned. Add the spicy sausage and green pepper and stir-fry for a further 3 minutes.

4 Add the cold rice and the sweetcorn to the wok and stir-fry for 2 minutes, then return the cooked sausages to the wok

and stir over the heat until everything is piping hot. Garnish with the freshly chopped parsley and serve immediately with a little grated mozzarella cheese.

HELPFUL HINT

It is now possible to buy packets of bacon or pancetta lardons, but if these are unavailable, try to get bacon in a piece from a butcher or deli. Cut the bacon into 1 cm/½ inch slices then cut the slices crossways into 1 cm/½ inch pieces.

SPEEDY PORK WITH YELLOW BEAN SAUCE

INGREDIENTS

Serves 4

450 g/1 lb pork fillet
2 tbsp light soy sauce
2 tbsp orange juice
2 tsp cornflour
3 tbsp groundnut oil
2 garlic cloves, peeled and
  crushed
175 g/6 oz carrots, peeled and
  cut into matchsticks
125 g/4 oz fine green beans,
  trimmed and halved

2 spring onions, trimmed and
  cut into strips
4 tbsp yellow bean sauce
1 tbsp freshly chopped flat leaf
  parsley, to garnish
freshly cooked egg noodles,
  to serve

1 Remove any fat or sinew from the pork fillet, and cut into thin strips. Blend the soy sauce, orange juice and cornflour in a bowl and mix thoroughly. Place the meat in a shallow dish, pour over the soy sauce mixture, cover and leave to marinate in the refrigerator for 1 hour. Drain with a slotted spoon, reserving the marinade.

2 Heat the wok, then add 2 tablespoons of the oil and stir-fry the pork with the garlic for 2 minutes, or until the meat is sealed. Remove with a slotted spoon and reserve.

3 Add the remaining oil to the wok and cook the carrots, beans and spring onions for about 3 minutes, until tender but still crisp. Return the pork to the wok with the reserved marinade, then pour over the yellow bean sauce. Stir-fry for a further 1–2 minutes, or until the pork is tender. Sprinkle with the chopped parsley and serve immediately with freshly cooked egg noodles.

FOOD FACT

Yellow bean sauce is available from either large supermarkets or Oriental grocers. It is one of many ready-made sauces commonly used in Chinese cookery. Black bean sauce may be substituted.

LAMB WITH BLACK CHERRY SAUCE

INGREDIENTS   Serves 4

550 g/1¼ lb lamb fillet
2 tbsp light soy sauce
1 tsp Chinese five spice powder
4 tbsp fresh orange juice
175 g/6 oz black cherry jam
150 ml/¼ pint red wine
50 g/2 oz fresh black cherries

1 tbsp groundnut oil
1 tbsp freshly chopped
  coriander, to garnish

TO SERVE:
thawed frozen peas
freshly cooked noodles

1 Remove the skin and any
fat from the lamb fillet and
cut into thin slices. Place in a
shallow dish. Mix together the
soy sauce, Chinese five spice
powder and orange juice and
pour over the meat. Cover and
leave in the refrigerator for at
least 30 minutes.

2 Meanwhile, blend the jam
and the wine together, pour
into a small saucepan and bring
to the boil. Simmer gently for 10
minutes until slightly thickened.
Remove the stones from the
cherries, using a cherry stoner
if possible in order to keep
them whole.

3 Drain the lamb when ready
to cook. Heat the wok, add
the oil and when the oil is hot,
stir-fry the slices of lamb for
3–5 minutes, or until just slightly
pink inside or cooked to personal
preference.

4 Spoon the lamb into a
warm serving dish and serve
immediately with a little of the

cherry sauce drizzled over.
Garnish with the chopped
coriander and the whole cherries
and serve immediately with peas,
freshly cooked noodles and the
remaining sauce.

TASTY TIP

Fresh cherries have
a very short season in
early summer, so if you want
to make this dish at other
times, substitute canned
or bottled cherries in juice.
Drain them well before
adding to the sauce.

HONEY PORK WITH RICE NOODLES & CASHEWS

INGREDIENTS

Serves 4

125 g/4 oz rice noodles
450 g/1 lb pork fillet
2 tbsp groundnut oil
1 tbsp softened butter
1 onion, peeled and finely
  sliced into rings
2 garlic cloves, peeled and
  crushed
125 g/4 oz baby button
  mushrooms, halved
3 tbsp light soy sauce

3 tbsp clear honey
50 g/2 oz unsalted cashew
  nuts
1 red chilli, deseeded and
  finely chopped
4 spring onions, trimmed
  and finely chopped
freshly stir-fried vegetables,
  to serve

1 Soak the rice noodles in boiling water for 4 minutes or according to packet instructions, then drain and reserve.

2 Trim and slice the pork fillet into thin strips. Heat the wok, pour in the oil and butter, and stir-fry the pork for 4–5 minutes, until cooked. Remove with a slotted spoon and keep warm.

3 Add the onion to the wok and stir-fry gently for 2 minutes. Stir in the garlic and mushrooms and cook for a further 2 minutes, or until juices start to run from the mushrooms.

4 Blend the soy sauce with the honey then return the pork to the wok with this mixture. Add the cashew nuts and cook for 1–2 minutes, then add the rice noodles a little at a time. Stir-

fry until everything is piping hot. Sprinkle with chopped chilli and spring onions. Serve immediately with freshly stir-fried vegetables.

TASTY TIP

Heat a wok until really hot, then add 1 tablespoon of oil. Carefully swirl around the wok, then add 1 chopped garlic clove and a little grated ginger. Add a finely sliced red, green and yellow pepper, some mangetout and spring onion. Stir-fry for 3–4 minutes, then serve with the pork.

SWEET-&-SOUR PORK

INGREDIENTS

Serves 4

450 g/1 lb pork fillet
1 medium egg white
4 tsp cornflour
salt and freshly ground black
 pepper
300 ml/½ pint groundnut oil
1 small onion, peeled and
 finely sliced
125 g/4 oz carrots, peeled and
 cut into matchsticks

2.5 cm/1 inch piece fresh root
 ginger, peeled and cut into
 thin strips
150 ml/¼ pint orange juice
150 ml/¼ pint chicken stock
1 tbsp light soy sauce
220 g can pineapple pieces,
 drained with juice reserved
1 tbsp white wine vinegar
1 tbsp freshly chopped parsley
freshly cooked rice, to serve

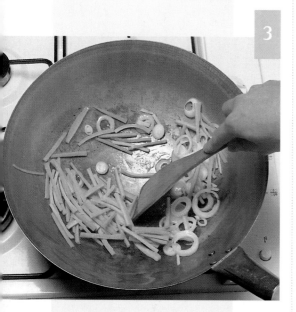

1 Trim, then cut the pork fillet into small cubes. In a bowl, whisk the egg white and cornflour with a little seasoning, then add the pork to the egg white mixture and stir until the cubes are well coated.

2 Heat the wok, then add the oil and heat until very hot before adding the pork and stir-frying for 30 seconds. Turn off the heat and continue to stir for 3 minutes. The meat should be white and sealed. Drain off the oil, reserve the pork and wipe the wok clean.

3 Pour 2 teaspoons of the drained groundnut oil back into the wok and cook the onion, carrots and ginger for 2–3 minutes. Blend the orange juice with the chicken stock and soy sauce and make up to 300 ml/½ pint with the reserved pineapple juice.

4 Return the pork to the wok with the juice mixture and simmer for 3–4 minutes. Then stir in the pineapple pieces and vinegar. Heat through, then sprinkle with the chopped parsley and serve immediately with freshly cooked rice.

TASTY TIP

If preferred, the pineapple pieces can be replaced with 1 large orange that has been peeled, segmented and roughly chopped.

CHILLI LAMB

INGREDIENTS   Serves 4

550 g/1¼ lb lamb fillet
3 tbsp groundnut oil
1 large onion, peeled and
   finely sliced
2 garlic cloves, peeled and
   crushed
4 tsp cornflour
4 tbsp hot chilli sauce
2 tbsp white wine vinegar
4 tsp dark soft brown sugar
1 tsp Chinese five spice powder

sprigs of fresh coriander, to
garnish

TO SERVE:
freshly cooked noodles
4 tbsp Greek style yogurt

1 Trim the lamb fillet, discarding any fat or sinew, then place it on a clean chopping board and cut into thin strips. Heat a wok and pour in 2 tablespoons of the groundnut oil and when hot, stir-fry the lamb for 3–4 minutes, or until it is browned. Remove the lamb strips with their juices and reserve.

2 Add the remaining oil to the wok, then stir-fry the onion and garlic for 2 minutes, or until softened. Remove with a slotted spoon and add to the lamb.

3 Blend the cornflour with 125 ml/4 fl oz of cold water, then stir in the chilli sauce, vinegar, sugar and Chinese five spice powder. Pour this into the wok, turn up the heat and bring the mixture to the boil. Cook for 30 seconds or until the sauce thickens.

4 Return the lamb to the wok with the onion and garlic, stir thoroughly and heat through until piping hot. Garnish with sprigs of fresh coriander and serve immediately with freshly cooked noodles, topped with a spoonful of Greek yogurt.

TASTY TIP

It is important to use bottled hot chilli sauce rather than Tabasco in this recipe. Chilli sauce is less fiery, though still quite hot, so taste a tiny bit first, then adjust the quantity according to taste.

SPICY LAMB IN YOGURT SAUCE

INGREDIENTS   Serves 4

1 tsp hot chilli powder
1 tsp ground cinnamon
1 tsp medium hot curry
  powder
1 tsp ground cumin
salt and freshly ground black
  pepper
2 tbsp groundnut oil
450 g/1 lb lamb fillet, trimmed
4 cardamom pods, bruised
4 whole cloves
1 onion, peeled and finely
  sliced
2 garlic cloves, peeled and
  crushed

2.5 cm/1 inch piece fresh root
  ginger, peeled and grated
150 ml/¼ pint Greek style
  yogurt
1 tbsp freshly chopped
  coriander
2 spring onions, trimmed and
  finely sliced

TO SERVE:
freshly cooked rice
naan bread

1 Blend the chilli powder, cinnamon, curry powder, cumin and seasoning with 2 tablespoons of the oil in a bowl and reserve. Cut the lamb fillet into thin strips, add to the spice and oil mixture and stir until coated thoroughly. Cover and leave to marinate in the refrigerator for at least 30 minutes.

2 Heat the wok, then pour in the remaining oil. When hot, add the cardamom pods and cloves and stir-fry for 10 seconds. Add the onion, garlic and ginger to the wok and stir fry for 3–4 minutes until softened.

3 Add the lamb with the marinading ingredients and stir-fry for a further 3 minutes

until cooked. Pour in the yogurt, stir thoroughly and heat until piping hot. Sprinkle with the chopped coriander and sliced spring onions then serve immediately with freshly cooked rice and naan bread.

HELPFUL HINT

Whole spices retain their freshness far longer than ready-ground ones. It is therefore preferable to buy whole spices in small quantities and grind them in a clean coffee grinder or spice grinder as they are needed.

PORK IN PEANUT SAUCE

INGREDIENTS   Serves 4

450 g/1 lb pork fillet
2 tbsp light soy sauce
1 tbsp vinegar
1 tsp sugar
1 tsp Chinese five spice
  powder
2–4 garlic cloves, peeled
  and crushed
2 tbsp groundnut oil
1 large onion, peeled and
  finely sliced
125 g/4 oz carrots, peeled and
  cut into matchsticks

2 celery sticks, trimmed and
  sliced
125 g/4 oz French beans,
  trimmed and halved
3 tbsp smooth peanut butter
1 tbsp freshly chopped flat leaf
  parsley

TO SERVE:
freshly cooked basmati and
  wild rice
green salad

1 Remove any fat or sinew from the pork fillet, cut into thin strips and reserve. Blend the soy sauce, vinegar, sugar, Chinese five spice powder and garlic in a bowl and add the pork. Cover and leave to marinate in the refrigerator for at least 30 minutes.

2 Drain the pork, reserving any marinade. Heat the wok, then add the oil and, when hot, stir-fry the pork for 3–4 minutes, or until sealed.

3 Add the onion, carrots, celery and beans to the wok and stir-fry for 4–5 minutes, or until the meat is tender and the vegetables are softened.

4 Blend the reserved marinade, the peanut butter and 2 tablespoons of hot water together. When smooth, stir into the wok and cook for several minutes more until the sauce is thick and the pork is piping hot. Sprinkle with the chopped parsley and serve immediately with the basmati and wild rice and a green salad.

TASTY TIP

For a tasty starter or canapé idea, leave the pork in peanut sauce to cool slightly, then serve wrapped in small, crisp lettuce leaves, such as iceberg.

STIR-FRIED BEEF WITH VERMOUTH

INGREDIENTS   Serves 4

350 g/12 oz beef steak, such as rump or sirloin

2 tbsp plain flour

salt and freshly ground black pepper

3 tbsp sunflower oil

2 shallots, peeled and finely chopped

125 g/4 oz button mushrooms, wiped and halved

2 tbsp freshly chopped tarragon

3 tbsp dry vermouth

150 ml/¼ pint single cream

125 g/4 oz stir-fry noodles

2 tsp sesame oil

1 Trim the beef and cut into thin strips. Place the flour in a bowl and add salt and pepper to taste, then stir well. Add the beef and stir until well coated, then remove from the flour and reserve.

2 Heat a wok, then add the oil and when hot, add the shallots and stir-fry for 2 minutes. Add the beef strips and stir-fry for 3–4 minutes before adding the mushrooms and 1 tablespoon of the chopped tarragon. Stir-fry for a further 1 minute.

3 Pour in the vermouth or Martini, stirring continuously, then add the cream. Cook for 2–3 minutes, or until the sauce is slightly thickened and the meat is cooked thoroughly. Adjust the seasoning and keep warm.

4 Meanwhile, place the noodles in a saucepan and cover with boiling water. Leave to stand for 4 minutes, then drain thoroughly and return to the wok. Add the sesame oil to the noodles and stir-fry for 1–2 minutes, or until heated through thoroughly. Pile the noodles onto serving dishes, top with the beef and serve immediately.

FOOD FACT

Vermouth is made using wormwood. The word 'vermouth' may, in fact, be a French corruption of 'wormwood'. Wormwood is also used in the production of absinthe.

PORK WITH SPRING VEGETABLES & SWEET CHILLI SAUCE

INGREDIENTS   Serves 4

450 g/16 oz pork fillet	2 tbsp sweet chilli sauce
2 tbsp sunflower oil	2 tbsp light soy sauce
2 garlic cloves, peeled and crushed	1 tbsp vinegar
2.5 cm/1 inch piece fresh root ginger, peeled and grated	½ tsp sugar, or to taste
125 g/4 oz carrots, peeled and cut into matchsticks	125 g/4 oz beansprouts
4 spring onions, trimmed	grated zest of 1 orange
125 g/4 oz sugar snap peas	freshly cooked rice, to serve
125 g/4 oz baby sweetcorn	

1 Trim, then cut the pork fillet into thin strips and reserve. Heat a wok and pour in the oil. When hot, add the garlic and ginger and stir-fry for 30 seconds. Add the carrots to the wok and continue to stir-fry for 1–2 minute, or until they start to soften.

2 Slice the spring onions lengthways, then cut into 3 lengths. Trim the sugar snap peas and the sweetcorn. Add the spring onions, sugar snap peas and sweetcorn to the wok and stir-fry for 30 seconds.

3 Add the pork to the wok and continue to stir-fry for 2–3 minutes, or until the meat is sealed and browned all over. Blend the sweet chilli sauce, soy sauce, vinegar and sugar together, then stir into the wok with the beansprouts.

4 Continue to stir-fry until the meat is cooked and the vegetables are tender but still crisp. Sprinkle with the orange zest and serve immediately with the freshly cooked rice.

TASTY TIP

It is tempting to assume that sweet chilli sauce is not hot, but it can still have a good chilli kick. It is wise to taste a little before adding it to the sauce and adjust the quantity according to taste.

BEEF WITH PAPRIKA

INGREDIENTS

Serves 4

700 g/1½ lb rump steak
3 tbsp plain flour
salt and freshly ground
  black pepper
1 tbsp paprika
350 g/12 oz long-grain
  rice
75 g/3 oz butter
1 tsp oil
1 onion, peeled and thinly
  sliced into rings

225 g/8 oz button mushrooms,
  wiped and sliced
2 tsp dry sherry
150 ml/¼ pint soured cream
2 tbsp freshly snipped chives
bundle of chives, to garnish

1 Beat the steak until very thin, then trim off and discard the fat and cut into thin strips. Season the flour with the salt, pepper and paprika, then toss the steak in the flour until coated.

2 Meanwhile, place the rice in a saucepan of boiling salted water and simmer for 15 minutes until tender or according to packet directions. Drain the rice, then return to the saucepan, add 25 g/1 oz of the butter, cover and keep warm.

3 Heat the wok, then add the oil and 25 g/1 oz of the butter. When hot, stir-fry the meat for 3–5 minutes until sealed. Remove from the wok with a slotted spoon and reserve. Add the remaining butter to the wok and stir-fry the onion rings and button mushrooms for 3–4 minutes.

4 Add the sherry while the wok is very hot, then turn down the heat. Return the steak to the wok with the soured cream and seasoning to taste. Heat through until piping hot, then sprinkle with the snipped chives. Garnish with bundles of chives and serve immediately with the cooked rice.

TASTY TIP

The button mushrooms in this recipe could be replaced by exotic or wild mushrooms. Chanterelles go particularly well with beef, as do ceps.

FRIED RICE WITH CHILLI BEEF

INGREDIENTS   Serves 4

225 g/8 oz beef fillet
375 g/12 oz long-grain rice
4 tbsp groundnut oil
3 onions, peeled and thinly
   sliced
2 hot red chillies, deseeded
   and finely chopped
2 tbsp light soy sauce
2 tsp tomato paste
salt and freshly ground black
   pepper

2 tbsp milk
2 tbsp flour
15 g/ ½ oz butter
2 medium eggs

1 Trim the beef fillet, discarding any fat, then cut into thin strips and reserve. Cook the rice in boiling salted water for 15 minutes or according to packet directions, then drain and reserve.

2 Heat a wok and add 3 tablespoons of oil. When hot, add 2 of the sliced onions and stir-fry for 2–3 minutes. Add the beef to the wok, together with the chillies, and stir-fry for a further 3 minutes, or until tender.

3 Add the rice to the wok with the soy sauce and tomato paste. Stir-fry for 1–2 minutes, or until piping hot. Season to taste with salt and pepper and keep warm. Meanwhile, toss the remaining onion in the milk, then the flour in batches. In a small frying pan fry the onion in the last 1 tablespoon of oil until crisp, then reserve.

4 Melt the butter in a small omelette pan. Beat the eggs with 2 teaspoons of water and pour into the pan. Cook gently, stirring frequently, until the egg has set, forming an omelette, then slide onto a clean chopping board and cut into thin strips. Add to the fried rice, sprinkle with the crispy onion and serve immediately.

HELPFUL HINT

To determine how hot a chilli is, the rule of thumb is 'the smaller the chilli, the hotter it is'. Small Thai bird's-eye chillies are extremely hot and should be used very sparingly.

LAMB'S LIVER WITH BACON & ONIONS

INGREDIENTS

Serves 4

350 g/12 oz lamb's liver
2 heaped tbsp plain flour
salt and freshly ground
 black pepper
2 tbsp groundnut oil
2 large onions, peeled and
 finely sliced
2 garlic cloves, peeled and
 chopped
1 red chilli, deseeded and
 chopped
175 g/6 oz streaky bacon

40 g/1½ oz butter
300 ml/½ pint lamb or
 beef stock
2 tbsp freshly chopped parsley

TO SERVE:
freshly cooked creamy
 mashed potatoes
freshly cooked green
 vegetables
freshly cooked carrots

1 Trim the liver, discarding any sinew or tubes, and thinly slice. Season the flour with salt and pepper, then use to coat the liver; reserve.

2 Heat a wok, then add the oil and when hot, add the sliced onion, garlic and chilli and cook for 5–6 minutes, or until soft and browned. Remove from the wok with a slotted spoon and reserve. Cut each slice of the bacon in half and stir-fry for 3–4 minutes or, until cooked. Remove with a slotted spoon and add to the onions.

3 Melt the butter in the wok and fry the liver on all sides until browned and crisp. Pour in the stock and allow to bubble fiercely for 1–2 minutes. Return the onions and bacon to the wok, stir thoroughly, then cover. Simmer gently for 10 minutes, or until the liver is tender. Sprinkle with the parsley and serve immediately with mashed potatoes and green vegetables and carrots.

TASTY TIP

For creamy mashed potatoes, peel and cube 450 g/1 lb floury potatoes. Cover with cold water and add salt. Bring to the boil and simmer for 15–20 minutes until tender. Drain well and return to the heat for a few seconds to dry out. Add 50 g/ 2 oz butter and 4 tablespoons of full cream milk and season. Mash thoroughly, adding a little more milk if necessary, until smooth and creamy.

SHREDDED BEEF IN HOISIN SAUCE

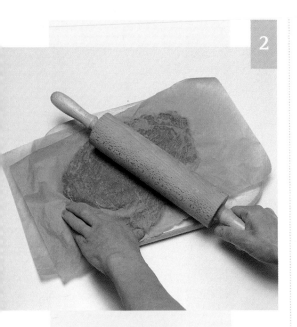

INGREDIENTS   Serves 4

2 celery sticks
125 g/4 oz carrots
450 g/1 lb rump steak
2 tbsp cornflour
salt and freshly ground
    black pepper
2 tbsp sunflower oil
4 spring onions, trimmed
    and chopped

2 tbsp light soy sauce
1 tbsp hoisin sauce
1 tbsp sweet chilli sauce
2 tbsp dry sherry
250 g pack fine egg thread
    noodles
1 tbsp freshly chopped
coriander

1 Trim the celery and peel the carrots, then cut into fine matchsticks and reserve.

2 Place the steak between 2 sheets of greaseproof paper or baking parchment. Beat the steak with a meat mallet or rolling pin until very thin, then slice into strips. Season the cornflour with salt and pepper and use to coat the steak. Reserve.

3 Heat a wok, add the oil and when hot, add the spring onions and cook for 1 minute, then add the steak and stir-fry for a further 3–4 minutes, or until the meat is sealed.

4 Add the celery and carrot matchsticks to the wok and stir-fry for a further 2 minutes before adding the soy, hoisin and chilli sauces and the sherry. Bring to the boil and simmer for 2–3 minutes, or until the steak is tender and the vegetables are cooked.

5 Plunge the fine egg noodles into boiling water and leave for 4 minutes. Drain, then spoon onto a large serving dish. Top with the cooked shredded steak, then sprinkle with chopped coriander and serve immediately.

TASTY TIP

Although this recipe calls for dry sherry, Chinese rice wine may be substituted if you can find it.

PORK WITH ASSORTED PEPPERS

INGREDIENTS   Serves 4

450 g/1 lb pork fillet
2 tbsp groundnut oil
1 onion, peeled and thinly
   sliced
1 red pepper, deseeded and
   cut into strips
1 yellow pepper, deseeded
   and cut into strips
1 orange pepper, deseeded
   and cut into strips
2 garlic cloves, peeled and
   crushed

2 tsp paprika
400 g can chopped tomatoes
300 ml/½ pint pork or chicken
   stock
1 tsp soft dark brown sugar
salt and freshly ground black
   pepper
handful fresh oregano leaves
350 g/12 oz penne
2 tbsp grated mozzarella
   cheese

1 Trim the pork fillet, discarding any sinew and fat, then cut into small cubes. Heat the wok, add the oil and, when hot, stir-fry the pork for 3–4 minutes until they are brown and sealed. Remove the pork from the wok and reserve.

2 Add the sliced onions to the wok and stir-fry until they are softened, but not browned, then add the pepper strips and stir-fry for a further 3–4 minutes.

3 Stir in the garlic, paprika, chopped tomatoes, stock, sugar and seasoning and bring to the boil. Simmer, uncovered, stirring occasionally, for 15 minutes, or until the sauce has reduced and thickened. Return the pork to the wok and simmer for a further 5–10 minutes. Sprinkle with the oregano leaves.

4 Cook the pasta for 3–4 minutes until 'al dente' or according to packet directions, then drain and serve immediately with the pork and grated mozzarella cheese.

TASTY TIP

Fresh oregano has a fairly powerful flavour, very similar to that of marjoram.
1 teaspoon of dried oregano may be used if preferred.

Beef Curry with Lemon & Arborio Rice

INGREDIENTS   Serves 4

450 g/1 lb beef fillet
1 tbsp olive oil
2 tbsp green curry paste
1 green pepper, deseeded and
  cut into strips
1 red pepper, deseeded
  and cut into strips
1 celery stick, trimmed and
  sliced
juice of 1 fresh lemon
2 tsp Thai fish sauce

2 tsp demerara sugar
225 g/8 oz Arborio rice
15 g/ ½ oz butter
2 tbsp freshly chopped
  coriander
4 tbsp crème fraîche

1 Trim the beef fillet, discarding any fat, then cut across the grain into thin slices. Heat a wok, add the oil and when hot, add the green curry paste and cook for 30 seconds. Add the beef strips and stir-fry for 3–4 minutes.

2 Add the sliced peppers and the celery and continue to stir-fry for 2 minutes. Add the lemon juice, Thai fish sauce and sugar and cook for a further 3–4 minutes, or until the beef is tender and cooked to personal preference.

3 Meanwhile, cook the Arborio rice in a saucepan of lightly salted boiling water for 15–20 minutes, or until tender. Drain, rinse with boiling water and drain again. Return to the saucepan and add the butter. Cover and allow the butter to melt before turning it out onto a large serving dish. Sprinkle the cooked curry with the chopped coriander and serve immediately with the rice and crème fraîche.

TASTY TIP

Fresh green curry paste can be made at home. Using a blender or spice grinder, finely chop together 3–4 deseeded hot green chillies, 1 lemon grass stalk, 2 shallots, 3 garlic cloves, 2.5 cm/1 inch piece galangal or ginger, 1 teaspoon ground coriander, ½ teaspoon ground cumin, 2 kaffir lime leaves and a handful of fresh coriander. Keep in the refrigerator.

LEMON CHICKEN

INGREDIENTS   Serves 4

450 g/1 lb skinless, boneless
  chicken breast fillets, cubed
1 medium egg white, beaten
1 tsp salt
1 tbsp sesame oil
1 tbsp cornflour
200 ml/7 fl oz groundnut oil
75 ml/3 fl oz chicken stock
zest and juice of 1 lemon
1 tbsp caster sugar
1 tbsp light soy sauce

2 tbsp Chinese rice wine or
  dry sherry
3 large garlic cloves, peeled
  and finely chopped
1–2 tsp dried red chillies,
  crushed
shredded fresh red chillies, to
  garnish
freshly steamed white rice, to
  serve

1 Place the cubes of chicken in a large bowl then add the beaten egg white, salt, 1 teaspoon of sesame oil and 1 teaspoon of cornflour. Mix lightly together until all the chicken is coated, then chill in the refrigerator for 20 minutes.

2 Heat the wok until very hot and add the oil. When hot, remove the wok from the heat and add the chicken. Stir-fry for 2 minutes, or until the chicken turns white, then remove with a slotted spoon and drain on absorbent kitchen paper.

3 Wipe the wok clean and heat it until hot again. Add the stock, lemon zest and juice, sugar, soy sauce, Chinese rice wine or sherry, garlic and crushed chillies and bring to the boil. Blend the remaining cornflour to a smooth paste with 1 tablespoon of water and add to the wok. Stir, then

simmer for 1 minute. Add the chicken cubes and stir-fry for 2–3 minutes. Add the remaining sesame oil, garnish with shredded chillies and serve immediately with freshly steamed rice.

HELPFUL HINT

If possible, use unwaxed lemons for this dish and for any dish using lemon zest. If these are unavailable, pour hot water over the lemons, then scrub them to remove the wax.

CHICKEN IN BLACK BEAN SAUCE

INGREDIENTS   Serves 4

450 g/1 lb skinless, boneless
    chicken breast fillets, cut into
    strips
1 tbsp light soy sauce
2 tbsp Chinese rice wine or
    dry sherry
salt
1 tsp caster sugar
1 tsp sesame oil
2 tsp cornflour
2 tbsp sunflower oil
2 green peppers, deseeded
    and diced
1 tbsp freshly grated root ginger

2 garlic cloves, peeled and
    roughly chopped
2 shallots, peeled and finely
    chopped
4 spring onions, trimmed and
    finely sliced
3 tbsp salted black beans,
    chopped
150 ml/¼ pint chicken stock
shredded spring onions, to
    garnish
freshly cooked egg noodles,
    to serve

1 Place the chicken strips in a large bowl. Mix together the soy sauce, Chinese rice wine or sherry, a little salt, caster sugar, sesame oil and cornflour and pour over the chicken.

2 Heat the wok over a high heat, add the oil and when very hot, add the chicken strips and stir-fry for 2 minutes. Add the green peppers and stir-fry for a further 2 minutes. Then add the ginger, garlic, shallots, spring onions and black beans and continue to stir-fry for another 2 minutes.

3 Add 4 tablespoons of the stock, stir-fry for 1 minute, then pour in the remaining stock and bring to the boil. Reduce the heat and simmer the sauce for 3–4 minutes, or until the chicken is cooked and the sauce has thickened slightly. Garnish with the shredded spring onions and serve immediately with noodles.

FOOD FACT

Black beans, also known as salted black beans, are soya beans that have been preserved by being fermented with salt and spices. They have a distinctive salty taste, a rich savoury aroma and are often used as a seasoning in conjunction with garlic or ginger. Buy the beans either in cans, in which case they will need rinsing and draining, or dry in bags. Dried black beans will keep indefinitely in an airtight container.

GREEN CHICKEN CURRY

INGREDIENTS   Serves 4

1 onion, peeled and chopped

3 lemon grass stalks, outer leaves discarded and finely sliced

2 garlic cloves, peeled and finely chopped

1 tbsp freshly grated root ginger

3 green chillies

zest and juice of 1 lime

2 tbsp groundnut oil

2 tbsp Thai fish sauce

6 tbsp freshly chopped coriander

6 tbsp freshly chopped basil

450 g/1 lb skinless, boneless chicken breasts, cut into strips

125 g /4 oz fine green beans, trimmed

400 ml can coconut milk

fresh basil leaves, to garnish

freshly cooked rice, to serve

1 Place the onion, lemon grass, garlic, ginger, chillies, lime zest and juice, 1 tablespoon of groundnut oil, the fish sauce, coriander and basil in a food processor. Blend to a form a smooth paste, which should be of a spoonable consistency. If the sauce looks thick, add a little water. Remove and reserve.

2 Heat the wok, add the remaining 1 tablespoon of oil and when hot add the chicken. Stir-fry for 2–3 minutes, until the chicken starts to colour, then add the green beans and stir-fry for a further minute. Remove the chicken and beans from the wok and reserve. Wipe the wok clean with absorbent kitchen paper.

3 Spoon the reserved green paste into the wok and heat for 1 minute. Add the coconut milk and whisk to blend. Return the chicken and beans to the wok and bring to the boil. Simmer for 5–7 minutes, or until the chicken is cooked. Sprinkle with basil leaves and serve immediately with freshly cooked rice.

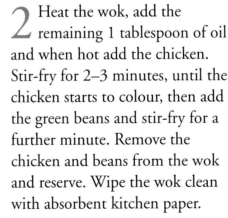

TASTY TIP

Use Thai holy basil in this recipe if possible. The leaves are flatter and coarser than Italian basil with a stronger, more pronounced aniseed flavour. Thai basil is available from Oriental grocers and some supermarkets.

CHICKEN CHOW MEIN

INGREDIENTS   Serves 4

225 g/8 oz egg noodles
5 tsp sesame oil
4 tsp light soy sauce
2 tbsp Chinese rice wine or
  dry sherry
salt and freshly ground black
  pepper
225 g/8 oz skinless chicken
  breast fillets, cut into strips
3 tbsp groundnut oil
2 garlic cloves, peeled and
  finely chopped

50 g/2 oz mangetout peas,
  finely sliced
50 g/2 oz cooked ham, cut into
  fine strips
2 tsp dark soy sauce
pinch of sugar

TO GARNISH:
shredded spring onions
toasted sesame seeds

1 Bring a large saucepan of water to the boil and add the noodles. Cook for 3–5 minutes, drain and plunge into cold water. Drain again, add 1 tablespoon of the sesame oil and stir lightly.

2 Place 2 teaspoons of light soy sauce, 1 tablespoon of Chinese rice wine or sherry, and 1 teaspoon of the sesame oil, with seasoning to taste in a bowl. Add the chicken and stir well. Cover lightly and leave to marinate in the refrigerator for about 15 minutes.

3 Heat the wok over a high heat, add 1 tablespoon of the groundnut oil and when very hot, add the chicken and its marinade and stir-fry for 2 minutes. Remove the chicken and juices and reserve. Wipe the wok clean with absorbent kitchen paper.

4 Reheat the wok and add the oil. Add the garlic and toss in the oil for 20 seconds. Add the mangetout peas and the ham and stir-fry for 1 minute. Add the noodles, remaining light soy sauce, Chinese rice wine or sherry, the dark soy sauce and sugar. Season to taste with salt and pepper and stir-fry for 2 minutes.

5 Add the chicken and juices to the wok and stir-fry for 4 minutes, or until the chicken is cooked. Drizzle over the remaining sesame oil. Garnish with spring onions and sesame seeds and serve.

FOOD FACT

Sesame oil is a thick, rich, golden brown oil made from toasted sesame seeds. It is used in Chinese cooking mainly as a seasoning.

CHICKEN SATAY SALAD

INGREDIENTS

Serves 4

4 tbsp crunchy peanut butter
1 tbsp chilli sauce
1 garlic clove, peeled and
   crushed
2 tbsp cider vinegar
2 tbsp light soy sauce
2 tbsp dark soy sauce
2 tsp soft brown sugar
pinch of salt
2 tsp freshly ground Sichuan
   peppercorns

450 g/1 lb dried egg noodles
2 tbsp sesame oil
1 tbsp groundnut oil
450 g/1 lb skinless, boneless
   chicken breast fillets, cut
   into cubes
shredded celery leaves, to
   garnish
cos lettuce, to serve

1 Place the peanut butter, chilli sauce, garlic, cider vinegar, soy sauces, sugar, salt and ground peppercorns in a food processor and blend to form a smooth paste. Scrape into a bowl, cover and chill in the refrigerator until required.

2 Bring a large saucepan of lightly salted water to the boil. Add the noodles and cook for 3–5 minutes. Drain and plunge into cold water. Drain again and toss in the sesame oil. Leave to cool.

3 Heat the wok until very hot, add the oil and when hot, add the chicken cubes. Stir-fry for 5–6 minutes until the chicken is golden brown and cooked through.

4 Remove the chicken from the wok using a slotted spoon and add to the noodles, together with the peanut sauce. Mix lightly together, then sprinkle with the shredded celery leaves and either serve immediately or leave until cold, then serve with cos lettuce.

FOOD FACT

Sichuan peppercorns are the dried berries of a shrub, which is a member of the citrus family. The smell is reminiscent of lavender and they have a sharp, mildly spicy flavour. They are often toasted in a dry frying pan before grinding, to bring out their distinctive flavour.

DUCK IN CRISPY WONTON SHELLS

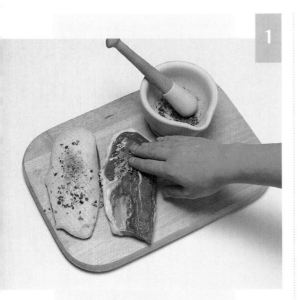

INGREDIENTS

Serves 4

2 x 175 g/6 oz duck breasts
2 tbsp Chinese five spice powder
2 tbsp Sichuan peppercorns
1 tsp whole black peppercorns
3 tbsp cumin seeds
5 tbsp sea salt
6 slices fresh root ginger
6 spring onions, roughly chopped

1 tbsp cornflour
1 litre/1¾ pints vegetable oil for frying
16 wonton wrappers
5 cm/2 inch piece cucumber, cut into fine strips
125 ml/4 fl oz hoisin sauce

1 Rinse the duck and dry thoroughly with absorbent kitchen paper. Place the Chinese five spice powder, peppercorns, cumin seeds and salt in a pestle and mortar and crush. Rub the spice mix all over the duck. Wrap in clingfilm and refrigerate for 24 hours.

2 Place a rack in the wok and pour in boiling water to a depth of 5 cm/2 inches. Place the duck breasts with the ginger slices and 3 chopped spring onions in a heatproof dish on top of the rack. Cover and steam for 40–50 minutes, or until the duck is cooked. Pour off any excess fat from time to time and add more water if necessary. Remove the duck and leave until cooled.

3 Dust the duck breasts with cornflour, shaking off the excess. Heat the wok, add the oil and, when almost smoking, deep-fry the duck for 8 minutes. Drain, then shred the meat into bite-sized pieces. Shred the remaining spring onions.

4 Reheat the oil until smoking. Working with 1 wonton at a time, insert 2 wooden skewers into each one, hold in a taco shape and lower into the oil. Hold in the oil until crisp and golden brown. Drain on absorbent kitchen paper. Repeat with the remaining wontons. Fill the wontons with the duck, topped with the spring onions, cucumber and hoisin sauce and serve immediately.

FOOD FACT

Chinese five spice powder contains star anise, Sichuan pepper, fennel, cloves and cinnamon.

CHICKEN & BABY VEGETABLE STIR FRY

INGREDIENTS

Serves 4

2 tbsp groundnut oil
1 small red chilli, deseeded
   and finely chopped
150 g/5 oz chicken breast
   or thigh meat, skinned and
   cut into cubes
2 baby leeks, trimmed and
   sliced
12 asparagus spears, halved
125 g/4 oz mangetout peas,
   trimmed
125 g/4 oz baby carrots,
   trimmed and halved
   lengthways
125 g/4 oz fine green beans,
   trimmed and diagonally
   sliced

125 g/4 oz baby sweetcorn,
   diagonally halved
50 ml/2 fl oz chicken stock
2 tsp light soy sauce
1 tbsp dry sherry
1 tsp sesame oil
toasted sesame seeds, to
   garnish

1 Heat the wok until very hot and add the oil. Add the chopped chilli and chicken and stir-fry for 4–5 minutes, or until the chicken is cooked and golden.

2 Increase the heat, add the leeks to the chicken and stir-fry for 2 minutes. Add the asparagus spears, mangetout peas, baby carrots, green beans, and baby sweetcorn. Stir-fry for 3–4 minutes, or until the vegetables soften slightly but still retain a slight crispness.

3 In a small bowl, mix together the chicken stock, soy sauce, dry sherry and sesame oil. Pour into the wok, stir and cook until heated through. Sprinkle with the toasted sesame seeds and serve immediately.

HELPFUL HINT

Look for packs of mixed baby vegetables in the supermarket. They are often available ready-trimmed and will save a lot of time.

SWEET-&-SOUR TURKEY

INGREDIENTS   Serves 4

2 tbsp groundnut oil
2 garlic cloves, peeled and
   chopped
1 tbsp freshly grated root
   ginger
4 spring onions, trimmed and
   cut into 4 cm/1½ inch lengths
450 g/1 lb turkey breast,
   skinned and cut into strips
1 red pepper, deseeded and
   cut into 2.5 cm/1 inch squares

225 g/8 oz canned water
   chestnuts, drained
150 ml/¼ pint chicken stock
2 tbsp Chinese rice wine
3 tbsp light soy sauce
2 tsp dark soy sauce
2 tbsp tomato paste
2 tbsp white wine vinegar
1 tbsp sugar
1 tbsp cornflour
egg-fried rice, to serve

1 Heat the wok over a high heat, add the oil and when hot, add the garlic, ginger and spring onions, stir-fry for 20 seconds.

2 Add the turkey to the wok and stir-fry for 2 minutes, or until beginning to colour. Add the peppers and water chestnuts and stir-fry for a further 2 minutes.

3 Mix the chicken stock, Chinese rice wine, light and dark soy sauce, tomato paste, white wine vinegar and the sugar together in a small jug or bowl. Add the mixture to the wok, stir and bring the sauce to the boil.

4 Mix together the cornflour with 2 tablespoons of water and add to the wok. Reduce the heat and simmer for 3 minutes, or until the turkey is cooked thoroughly and the sauce slightly thickened and glossy. Serve immediately with egg-fried rice.

TASTY TIP

To make egg-fried rice, heat 1 tablespoon vegetable oil in a clean wok. Add 450 g/1 lb cold cooked rice and stir-fry briefly before adding 125 g/ 4 oz thawed frozen peas. Stir-fry for a further 5 minutes over a high heat. Add 2 medium beaten eggs and 125 g/ 4 oz beansprouts and cook for a further 2 minutes until the eggs have set. Turn the mixture onto a plate and garnish with 2 finely chopped spring onions. Serve immediately.

THAI COCONUT CHICKEN

INGREDIENTS

Serves 4

1 tsp cumin seeds
1 tsp mustard seeds
1 tsp coriander seeds
1 tsp turmeric
1 bird's-eye chilli, deseeded and finely chopped
1 tbsp freshly grated root ginger
2 garlic cloves, peeled and finely chopped
125 ml/4 fl oz double cream
8 skinless chicken thighs

2 tbsp groundnut oil
1 onion, peeled and finely sliced
200 ml/7 fl oz coconut milk
salt and freshly ground black pepper
4 tbsp freshly chopped coriander
2 spring onions, shredded, to garnish
freshly cooked Thai fragrant rice, to serve

1 Heat the wok and add the cumin seeds, mustard seeds and coriander seeds. Dry-fry over a low to medium heat for 2 minutes, or until the fragrance becomes stronger and the seeds start to pop. Add the turmeric and leave to cool slightly. Grind the spices in a pestle and mortar or blend to a fine powder in a food processor.

2 Mix the chilli, ginger, garlic and the cream together in a small bowl, add the ground spices and mix. Place the chicken thighs in a shallow dish and spread the spice paste over the thighs.

3 Heat the wok over a high heat, add the oil and when hot, add the onion and stir-fry until golden brown. Add the chicken and spice paste. Cook for 5–6 minutes, stirring occasionally, until evenly coloured. Add the coconut milk and season to taste with salt and pepper. Simmer the chicken for 15–20 minutes, or until the thighs are cooked through, taking care not to allow the mixture to boil. Stir in the chopped coriander and serve immediately with the freshly cooked rice sprinkled with shredded spring onions.

TASTY TIP

Frying the spices before grinding them helps to release their essential oils. This, in turn, brings out the flavour of the spices, making them much more aromatic.

DEEP-FRIED CHICKEN WINGS

INGREDIENTS   Serves 4

2 tsp turmeric
1 tsp hot chilli powder
1 tsp ground coriander
1 tsp ground cumin
3 garlic cloves, peeled and
   crushed
8 chicken wings
2 tbsp orange marmalade
2 tbsp ginger preserve or
   marmalade
1 tsp salt

3 tbsp rice wine vinegar
2 tbsp tomato ketchup
1 litre/1¾ pints vegetable oil
   for deep frying
lime wedges, to garnish

1 Blend the turmeric, chilli powder, ground coriander, ground cumin and garlic together in a small bowl. Dry the chicken wings thoroughly, using absorbent kitchen paper, then rub the spice mixture onto the skin of each chicken wing. Cover and chill in the refrigerator for at least 2 hours.

2 Meanwhile make the dipping sauce, by mixing together the marmalade, ginger preserve, salt, rice wine vinegar and tomato ketchup in a small saucepan. Heat until blended, leave to cool, then serve. If using straight away, spoon into a small dipping bowl, but if using later pour into a container with a close-fitting lid and store in the refrigerator.

3 Pour the oil into the wok and heat to 190°C/375°F, or until a small cube of bread dropped in the oil turns golden brown in 30 seconds. Cook 2–3 chicken wings

at a time, lowering them into the hot oil, and frying for 3–4 minutes. Remove the wings, using a slotted spoon, and drain on absorbent kitchen paper. You may need to reheat the oil before cooking each batch.

4 When all the chicken wings are cooked, arrange on a warmed serving dish, garnish with the lime wedges and serve.

HELPFUL HINT

It is important to test the oil to make sure it is at the right temperature. If the oil is not hot enough, the chicken will be greasy but if it is too hot, the food may burn without being properly cooked through.

STIR-FRIED CHICKEN WITH BASIL

INGREDIENTS

Serves 4

3 tbsp sunflower oil
3 tbsp green curry paste
450 g/1 lb skinless, boneless
  chicken breast fillets,
  trimmed and cut into cubes
8 cherry tomatoes
100 ml/4 fl oz coconut cream
2 tbsp soft brown sugar
2 tbsp Thai fish sauce
1 red chilli, deseeded and
  thinly sliced

1 green chilli, deseeded and
  thinly sliced
75 g/3 oz fresh torn basil
  leaves
sprigs of fresh coriander, to
  garnish
freshly steamed white rice,
  to serve

1 Heat the wok, then add the oil and heat for 1 minute. Add the green curry paste and cook, stirring for 1 minute to release the flavour and cook the paste. Add the chicken and stir-fry over a high heat for 2 minutes, making sure the chicken is coated thoroughly with the green curry paste.

2 Reduce the heat under the wok, then add the cherry tomatoes and cook, stirring gently, for 2–3 minutes, or until the tomatoes burst and begin to disintegrate into the green curry paste.

3 Add half the coconut cream and add to the wok with the brown sugar, Thai fish sauce and the red and green chillies. Stir-fry gently for 5 minutes, or until the sauce is amalgamated and the chicken is cooked thoroughly.

4 Just before serving, sprinkle the chicken with the torn basil leaves and add the remaining coconut cream, then serve immediately with freshly steamed white rice garnished with fresh coriander sprigs.

FOOD FACT

Creamed coconut is a waxy block of hardened coconut cream. It is very high in fat but adds a rich creaminess to the dish. It can be chopped or grated and melts very easily on contact with the hot sauce.

NOODLES WITH TURKEY & MUSHROOMS

INGREDIENTS   Serves 4

225 g/8 oz dried egg noodles
1 tbsp groundnut oil
1 red onion, peeled and sliced
2 tbsp freshly grated root
   ginger
3 garlic cloves, peeled and
   finely chopped
350 g/12 oz turkey breast,
   skinned and cut into strips

125 g/4 oz baby button
   mushrooms
150 g/5 oz chestnut
   mushrooms
2 tbsp dark soy sauce
2 tbsp hoisin sauce
2 tbsp dry sherry
4 tbsp vegetable stock
2 tsp cornflour

1 Bring a large saucepan of lightly salted water to the boil and add the noodles. Cook for 3–5 minutes, then drain and plunge immediately into cold water. When cool, drain again and reserve.

2 Heat the wok, add the oil and when hot, add the onion and stir-fry for 3 minutes until it starts to soften. Add the ginger and garlic and stir-fry for a further 3 minutes, then add the turkey strips and stir-fry for 4–5 minutes until sealed and golden.

3 Wipe and slice the chestnut mushrooms into similar-sized pieces and add to the wok with the whole button mushrooms. Stir-fry for 3–4 minutes, or until tender. When all the vegetables are tender and the turkey is cooked, add the soy sauce, hoisin sauce, sherry and vegetable stock.

4 Mix the cornflour with 2 tablespoons of water and add to the wok, then cook, stirring, until the sauce thickens. Add the drained noodles to the wok, then toss the mixture together and serve immediately.

HELPFUL HINT

When buying wild mushrooms, choose dry-looking specimens without any soft spots. To prepare them, do not wash but brush away any dirt and wipe over gently with a damp cloth.

CHICKEN & CASHEW NUTS

INGREDIENTS   Serves 4

450 g/1 lb skinless chicken, boneless breast fillets, cut into 1 cm/½ inch cubes
1 medium egg white, beaten
1 tsp salt
1 tsp sesame oil
2 tsp cornflour
300 ml/½ pint groundnut oil for deep frying
2 tsp sunflower oil
50 g/2 oz unsalted cashews

4 spring onions, shredded
50 g/2 oz mangetout peas, diagonally sliced
1 tbsp Chinese rice wine
1 tbsp light soy sauce
shredded spring onions, to garnish
freshly steamed white rice with fresh coriander leaves, to serve

1 Place the cubes of chicken in a large bowl. Add the egg white, salt, sesame oil and cornflour. Mix well to ensure the chicken is coated thoroughly. Chill in the refrigerator for 20 minutes.

2 Heat the wok until very hot, add the groundnut oil and when hot, remove the wok from the heat and add the chicken. Stir continuously to prevent the chicken from sticking to the wok. When the chicken turns white, after about 2 minutes, remove it using a slotted spoon and reserve. Discard the oil.

3 Wipe the wok clean with absorbent kitchen paper and heat it again until very hot. Add the sunflower oil and heat. When hot, add the cashew nuts, spring onions and mangetout peas and stir-fry for 1 minute.

4 Add the rice wine and soy sauce. Return the chicken to the wok and stir-fry for 2 minutes. Garnish with shredded spring onions and serve immediately with freshly steamed rice sprinkled with fresh coriander.

FOOD FACT

Adding egg white mixed with cornflour to raw chicken is a classic Chinese technique called 'velveting'. It makes the chicken particularly tender. However, the egg white tends to stick to the wok, so the wok usually needs to be wiped clean between the different stages of cooking.

SZECHUAN TURKEY NOODLES

INGREDIENTS   Serves 4

1 tbsp tomato paste
2 tsp black bean sauce
2 tsp cider vinegar
salt and freshly ground black
  pepper
½ tsp Szechuan pepper
2 tsp sugar
4 tsp sesame oil
225 g/8 oz dried egg noodles
2 tbsp groundnut oil
2 tsp freshly grated root ginger

3 garlic cloves, peeled and
  roughly chopped
2 shallots, peeled and finely
  chopped
2 courgettes, trimmed and cut
  into fine matchsticks
450 g/1 lb turkey breast,
  skinned and cut into strips
deep-fried onion rings, to
  garnish

1 Mix together the tomato paste, black bean sauce, cider vinegar, a pinch of salt and pepper, the sugar and half the sesame oil. Chill in the refrigerator for 30 minutes.

2 Bring a large saucepan of lightly salted water to the boil and add the noodles. Cook for 3–5 minutes, drain and plunge immediately into cold water. Toss with the remaining sesame oil and reserve.

3 Heat the wok until very hot, then add the oil and when hot, add the ginger, garlic and shallots. Stir-fry for 20 seconds, then add the courgettes and turkey strips. Stir-fry for 3–4 minutes, or until the turkey strips are sealed.

4 Add the prepared chilled black bean sauce and continue to stir-fry for another 4 minutes over a high heat. Add the drained noodles to the wok and stir until the noodles, turkey, vegetables and the sauce are well mixed together. Garnish with the deep-fried onion rings and serve immediately.

FOOD FACT

Fresh ginger is indispensable as a flavouring in Chinese cookery. Its pungent, spicy, fresh taste adds a subtle but very distinctive flavour to all types of dishes. Root ginger looks rather like a gnarled Jerusalem artichoke and can vary in size. It has a pale brown, papery skin that is usually removed before use. Look for firm pieces with no signs of shrivelling. Keep root ginger wrapped in clingfilm in the refrigerator.

STIR-FRIED CHICKEN WITH SPINACH, TOMATOES & PINE NUTS

INGREDIENTS   Serves 4

50 g/2 oz pine nuts
2 tbsp sunflower oil
1 red onion, peeled and finely
    chopped
450 g/1 lb skinless, boneless
    chicken breast fillets, cut
    into strips
450 g/1 lb cherry tomatoes,
    halved
225 g/8 oz baby spinach,
    washed

salt and freshly ground black
    pepper
¼ tsp freshly grated nutmeg
2 tbsp balsamic vinegar
50 g/2 oz raisins
freshly cooked ribbon noodles
    tossed in butter, to serve

1 Heat the wok and add the pine nuts. Dry-fry for about 2 minutes, shaking often to ensure that they toast but do not burn. Remove and reserve. Wipe any dust from the wok.

2 Heat the wok again, add the oil and when hot, add the red onion and stir-fry for 2 minutes. Add the chicken and stir-fry for 2–3 minutes, or until golden brown. Reduce the heat, toss in the cherry tomatoes and stir-fry gently until the tomatoes start to disintegrate.

3 Add the baby spinach and stir-fry for 2–3 minutes, or until they start to wilt. Season to taste with salt and pepper, then sprinkle in the grated nutmeg and drizzle in the balsamic vinegar. Finally, stir in the raisins and reserved toasted pine nuts. Serve immediately on a bed of buttered ribbon noodles.

HELPFUL HINT

Baby spinach is available ready to use in bags, sold in most supermarkets. It has a more subtle, creamier flavour than larger-leaved spinach and cooks very quickly.

LIME & SESAME TURKEY

INGREDIENTS   Serves 4

450 g/1 lb turkey breast,
  skinned and cut into strips
2 lemon grass stalks, outer
  leaves discarded and finely
  sliced
grated zest of 1 lime
4 garlic cloves, peeled and
  crushed
6 shallots, peeled and finely
  sliced
2 tbsp Thai fish sauce

2 tsp soft brown sugar
1 small red chilli, deseeded
  and finely sliced
3 tbsp sunflower oil
1 tbsp sesame oil
225 g/8 oz stir-fry rice noodles
1 tbsp sesame seeds
shredded spring onions, to
  garnish
freshly stir-fried vegetables, to
  serve

1 Place the turkey strips in a shallow dish. Mix together the lemon grass stalks, lime zest, garlic, shallots, Thai fish sauce, sugar and chilli with 2 tablespoons of the sunflower oil and the sesame oil. Pour over the turkey. Cover and leave to marinate in the refrigerator for 2–3 hours, spooning the marinade over the turkey occasionally.

2 Soak the noodles in warm water for 5 minutes. Drain through a sieve or colander, then plunge immediately into cold water. Drain again and reserve until ready to use.

3 Heat the wok until very hot and add the sesame seeds. Dry-fry for 1–2 minutes, or until toasted in colour. Remove from the wok and reserve. Wipe the wok to remove any dust left from the seeds.

4 Heat the wok again and add the remaining sunflower oil. When hot, drain the turkey from the marinade and stir-fry for 3–4 minutes, or until golden brown and cooked through (you may need to do this in 2 batches). When all the turkey has been cooked, add the noodles to the wok and cook, stirring, for 1–2 minutes, or until heated through thoroughly. Garnish with the shredded spring onions, toasted sesame seeds and serve immediately with freshly stir-fried vegetables of your choice.

FOOD FACT

Lemon grass is a common ingredient in Thai cooking. It looks a little like a spring onion but has a distinctive lemony flavour. It keeps well for 2–3 weeks in the refrigerator.

HOISIN DUCK & GREENS STIR FRY

INGREDIENTS

Serves 4

350 g/12 oz duck breasts,
  skinned and cut
  into strips
1 medium egg white, beaten
½ tsp salt
1 tsp sesame oil
2 tsp cornflour
2 tbsp groundnut oil
2 tbsp freshly grated root
  ginger
50 g/2 oz bamboo shoots

50 g/2 oz fine green beans,
  trimmed
50 g/2 oz pak choi, trimmed
2 tbsp hoisin sauce
1 tsp Chinese rice wine or
  dry sherry
zest and juice of ½ orange
strips of orange zest, to
  garnish
freshly steamed egg noodles,
  to serve

1 Place the duck strips in a shallow dish, then add the egg white, salt, sesame oil and cornflour. Stir lightly until the duck is coated in the mixture. Cover and chill in the refrigerator for 20 minutes.

2 Heat the wok until very hot and add the oil. Remove the wok from the heat and add the duck, stirring continuously to prevent the duck from sticking to the wok. Add the ginger and stir-fry for 2 minutes. Add the bamboo shoots, the green beans and the pak choi, and stir-fry for 1–2 minutes until wilted.

3 Mix together the hoisin sauce, the Chinese rice wine or sherry and the orange zest and juice. Pour into the wok and stir to coat the duck and vegetables. Stir-fry for 1–2 minutes, or until the duck and vegetables are tender. Garnish with the strips of orange zest and serve immediately with freshly steamed egg noodles.

HELPFUL HINT

Duck breasts are usually sold with the skin on, but it is very easy to remove and all the fat usually comes away readily with the skin. If any remains, simply remove with a sharp knife.

DUCK & EXOTIC FRUIT STIR FRY

INGREDIENTS

Serves 4

4 duck breast fillets, skinned removed and cut into strips
½ tsp Chinese five spice powder
2 tbsp soy sauce
1 tbsp sesame oil
1 tbsp groundnut oil
2 celery stalks, trimmed and diced
225 g can pineapples chunks, drained

1 mango, peeled, stoned and cut into chunks
125 g/4 oz lychees, peeled if fresh, stoned and halved
125 ml/4 fl oz chicken stock
2 tbsp tomato paste
2 tbsp plum sauce
2 tsp wine vinegar
pinch of soft brown sugar
toasted nuts, to garnish
steamed rice, to serve

1 Place the duck strips in a shallow bowl. Mix together the Chinese five spice powder, soy sauce and sesame oil, pour over the duck and marinate for 2 hours in the refrigerator. Stir occasionally during marinating. Remove the duck from the marinade and reserve.

2 Heat the wok, add the oil and when hot, stir-fry the marinated duck strips for 4 minutes. Remove from the wok and reserve.

3 Add the celery to the wok and stir-fry for 2 minutes, then add the pineapple, mango and lychees and stir-fry for a further 3 minutes. Return the duck to the wok.

4 Mix together the chicken stock, tomato paste, plum sauce, wine vinegar and a pinch of brown sugar. Add to the wok,

bring to the boil and simmer, stirring, for 2 minutes. Sprinkle with the nuts and serve immediately with the freshly steamed rice.

TASTY TIP

The exotic fruit in this recipe not only looks beautiful, but helps to cut through the richness of the duck meat. Do not overcook the duck or it will become dry.

Teriyaki Duck with Plum Chutney

INGREDIENTS

Serves 4

4 tbsp Japanese soy sauce
4 tbsp dry sherry
2 garlic cloves, peeled and finely chopped
2.5 cm/1 inch piece fresh root ginger, peeled and finely chopped
350 g/12 oz skinless duck breast fillets, cut in chunks
2 tbsp groundnut oil
225 g/8 oz carrots, peeled and cut into fine strips
½ cucumber, cut into strips
5 spring onions, trimmed and shredded

toasted almonds, to garnish
freshly cooked egg noodles, to serve

FOR THE PLUM CHUTNEY:
25 g/1 oz butter
1 red onion, peeled and finely chopped
2 tsp soft brown sugar
4 plums, stoned and halved
zest and juice of ½ orange
50 g/2 oz raisins

1 Mix together the soy sauce, sherry, garlic and ginger and pour into a shallow dish. Add the duck strips and stir until coated in the marinade. Cover and leave in the refrigerator for 30 minutes.

2 Meanwhile make the plum chutney. Melt the butter in a wok, add the onion and sugar and cook gently over a low heat for 20 minutes. Add the plums, orange zest and juice and simmer for 10 minutes, then stir in the raisins. Spoon into a small bowl and wipe the wok clean. Drain the duck, reserving the marinade.

3 Heat the wok, add the oil and when hot, add the carrots, cucumber and spring onions.

Stir-fry for 2 minutes, or until tender. Remove and reserve.

4 Add the drained duck to the wok and stir-fry over a high heat for 2 minutes. Return the vegetables to the wok and add the reserved marinade. Stir-fry briefly, until heated through.

5 Garnish the duck with the toasted almonds and serve immediately with freshly cooked noodles and the plum chutney.

HELPFUL HINT

If the plum chutney is a bit runny, bring to the boil and cook for 5 minutes to thicken.

STEAMED, CRISPY, CITRUS CHICKEN

INGREDIENTS   Serves 6

200 ml/7 fl oz light soy sauce
1 tbsp brown sugar
4 star anise
2 slices fresh root ginger, peeled
5 spring onions, trimmed and sliced
1 small orange, cut into wedges
1 lime, cut into wedges

1.1 kg/2 ½ lb chicken
2 garlic cloves, peeled and finely chopped
2 tbsp Chinese rice wine
2 tbsp dark soy sauce
300 ml/½ pint groundnut oil
orange slices, to garnish
freshly cooked steamed rice, to serve

1 Pour the light soy sauce and 200 ml/7 fl oz water into the wok and add the sugar and star anise. Bring to the boil over a gentle heat. Pour into a small bowl and leave to cool slightly. Wipe the wok clean with absorbent kitchen paper.

2 Put the ginger, 2 spring onions, orange and lime inside the cavity of the chicken. Place a rack in the wok and pour in boiling water to a depth of 5 cm/2 inches. Put a piece of tinfoil onto the rack and place the chicken in the centre, then pour over the soy sauce mixture.

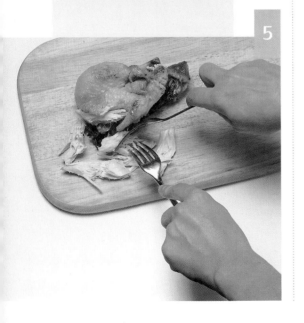

3 Cover the wok and steam gently for 1–1 hour 10 minutes, or until the chicken is cooked through, pouring off excess fat from time to time. Add more water if necessary. Leave the chicken to cool and dry for up to 3 hours, then cut the chicken into quarters.

4 Mix together the garlic, Chinese rice wine, dark soy sauce and remaining spring onions, then reserve. Dry the wok and heat again, then add the oil. When hot, shallow fry the chicken quarters for 4 minutes, or until golden and crisp. Do this 1 portion at a time, remove and drain on absorbent kitchen paper.

5 When cool enough to handle shred into bite-sized pieces and drizzle over the sauce. Garnish with slices of orange and serve with freshly steamed rice.

TASTY TIP

If you prefer, serve the shredded chicken with ready-made Chinese pancakes which have been spread with a little hoisin sauce. Top with shredded spring onions and cucumber and roll up.

THAI SPRING ROLLS WITH NOODLES & DIPPING SAUCE

INGREDIENTS

Makes about 30

50 g/2 oz dried rice vermicelli

1 carrot, peeled and cut into matchsticks

50 g/2 oz mangetout peas, thinly shredded lengthways

3 spring onions, trimmed and finely chopped

125 g/4 oz peeled prawns, thawed if frozen

2 garlic cloves, peeled and crushed

1 tsp sesame oil

2 tbsp light soy sauce

1 tsp chilli sauce

200 g/7 oz filo pastry, cut into 15 cm/6 inch squares

1 medium egg white, lightly beaten

vegetable oil for deep frying

sprigs of fresh coriander, to garnish

sweet chilli sauce, for dipping

1 Cook the rice vermicelli according to the packet directions, then drain thoroughly. Roughly chop and reserve. Bring a saucepan of lightly salted water to the boil and blanch the carrot and mangetout peas for 1 minute. Drain and refresh under cold water, then drain again and pat dry on absorbent kitchen paper. Mix together with the noodles. Add the spring onions, prawns, garlic, sesame oil, soy sauce and chilli sauce and reserve.

2 Fold the filo pastry squares in half diagonally to form triangles. Lay a triangle with the fold facing you and place a spoonful of the mixture in the centre. Roll over the long end of the wrapper to enclose the filling, then bring over the corners to enclose the ends of the roll. Brush the point of the spring roll furthest from you with a little beaten egg white and continue rolling to seal.

3 Fill a wok about a third full with vegetable oil and heat to 190°C/375°F, or until a cube of bread browns in 30 seconds. Fry the spring rolls, 4 or 5 at a time, for 1–2 minutes, or until golden and crisp. Drain on absorbent kitchen paper. Fry the remaining spring rolls in batches. Garnish with sprigs of coriander and serve hot with the dark soy sauce and sweet chilli sauce.

HELPFUL HINT

If available, use spring roll wrappers instead of filo pastry. Buy the larger sized ones and follow the recipe from step 2.

SINGAPORE NOODLES

INGREDIENTS
Serves 4

225 g/8 oz flat rice noodles
3 tbsp sunflower oil
2 shallots, peeled and sliced
2 garlic cloves, peeled and
  crushed
2 tbsp freshly grated root
  ginger
1 red pepper, deseeded and
  finely sliced
1 hot red chilli, deseeded and
  finely chopped

175 g/6 oz peeled raw prawns
125 g/4 oz boneless pork, diced
175 g/6 oz boneless chicken,
  diced
1 tbsp curry powder
1 tsp each crushed fennel
  seeds and ground cinnamon
50 g/2 oz frozen peas, thawed
juice of 1 lemon
3 tbsp fresh coriander leaves

1 Put the noodles into a large bowl and pour over boiling water to cover. Leave to stand for 3 minutes, or until slightly underdone according to the packet directions. Drain well and reserve.

2 Heat a wok until almost smoking. Add the oil and carefully swirl around to coat the sides of the wok. Add the shallots, garlic and ginger and cook for a few seconds. Add the pepper and chilli and stir-fry for 3–4 minutes, or until the pepper has softened.

3 Add the prawns, pork, chicken and curry powder to the wok. Stir-fry for a further 4–5 minutes until the meat and prawns are coloured on all sides. Then add the fennel seeds and the ground cinnamon and stir to mix.

4 Add the drained noodles to the wok along with the peas and cook for a further 1–2 minutes until heated through. Add the lemon juice to taste. Sprinkle with the fresh coriander leaves and serve immediately.

HELPFUL HINT

Use whatever meat or fish you prefer according to taste. This is also a great dish for using up leftover meat, perhaps from the Sunday roast. If using cooked meat, reduce the cooking time accordingly, but make sure that it is piping hot.

ORIENTAL NOODLE & PEANUT SALAD WITH CORIANDER

INGREDIENTS   Serves 4

350 g/12 oz rice vermicelli
1 litre/1¾ pints light chicken
   stock
2 tsp sesame oil
2 tbsp light soy sauce
8 spring onions
3 tbsp groundnut oil
2 hot green chillis, deseeded
   and thinly sliced
25 g/1 oz roughly chopped
   coriander

2 tbsp freshly chopped mint
125 g/4 oz cucumber, finely
   chopped
40 g/1½ oz beansprouts
40 g/1½ oz roasted peanuts,
   roughly chopped

1 Put the noodles into a large bowl. Bring the stock to the boil and immediately pour over the noodles. Leave to soak for 4 minutes, or according to the packet directions. Drain well, discarding the stock or saving it for another use. Mix together the sesame oil and soy sauce and pour over the hot noodles. Toss well to coat and leave until cold.

2 Trim and thinly slice 4 of the spring onions. Heat the oil in a wok over a low heat. Add the spring onions and, as soon as they sizzle, remove from the heat and leave to cool. When cold, toss with the noodles.

3 On a chopping board, cut the remaining spring onions lengthways 4–6 times, leave in a bowl of cold water until tassels form. Serve the noodles in individual bowls, each dressed with a little chilli, coriander, mint, cucumber, beansprouts and peanuts. Garnish with the spring onion tassels and serve.

HELPFUL HINT

To make this dish entirely vegetarian, cook the noodles in vegetable stock or water. If using water, be sure to add salt.

JAMBALAYAN-STYLE FRIED RICE

INGREDIENTS

Serves 6

450 g/1 lb long-grain rice
900 ml/1½ pints hot chicken or
  fish stock
2 fresh bay leaves
2 tbsp vegetable oil
2 medium onions, peeled and
  roughly chopped
1 green pepper, deseeded and
  roughly chopped
2 sticks celery, trimmed and
  roughly chopped
3 garlic cloves, peeled and
  finely chopped
1 tsp dried oregano

300 g/11 oz skinless chicken
  breast fillets, chopped
125 g/4 oz chorizo sausage,
  chopped
3 tomatoes, peeled and
  chopped
12 large raw prawns, peeled
  if preferred
4 spring onions, trimmed and
  finely chopped
2 tbsp freshly chopped parsley
salt and freshly ground black
  pepper

1 Put the rice, stock and bay leaves into a large saucepan and bring to the boil. Cover with a tight-fitting lid and simmer for 10 minutes over a very low heat. Remove from the heat and leave for a further 10 minutes.

2 Meanwhile, heat a large wok, then add the oil and heat. When hot, add the onions, green pepper, celery, garlic and oregano. Stir-fry for 6 minutes, or until all the vegetables have softened. Add the chicken and chorizo and stir-fry for a further 6 minutes, or until lightly browned.

3 Add the tomatoes and cook over a medium heat for 2–3 minutes until collapsed. Then stir in the prawns and cook for a further 4 minutes, or until they are cooked through. Stir in the cooked rice, spring onions and chopped parsley and season to taste with salt and pepper. Serve immediately.

TASTY TIP

Look for large, fat chorizo for this dish. The small, thin sausages are not authentic and have less flavour.

CHICKEN & RED PEPPER CURRIED RICE

INGREDIENTS   Serves 4

350 g/12 oz long-grain rice
salt
1 large egg white
1 tbsp cornflour
300 g/11 oz skinless chicken
  breast fillets, cut into chunks
3 tbsp groundnut oil
1 red pepper, deseeded and
  roughly chopped
1 tbsp curry powder or paste
125 ml/4 fl oz chicken stock

1 tsp sugar
1 tbsp Chinese rice wine or
  dry sherry
1 tbsp light soy sauce
sprigs of fresh coriander, to
  garnish

1 Wash the rice in several changes of water until the water remains relatively clear. Drain well. Put into a saucepan and cover with fresh water. Add a little salt and bring to the boil. Cook for 7–8 minutes until tender. Drain and refresh under cold running water, then drain again and reserve.

2 Lightly whisk the egg white with 1 teaspoon of salt and 2 teaspoons of cornflour until smooth. Add the chicken and mix together well. Cover and chill in the refrigerator for 20 minutes.

3 Heat the oil in a wok until moderately hot. Add the chicken mixture to the wok and stir-fry for 2–3 minutes until all the chicken has turned white. Using a slotted spoon, lift the cubes of chicken from the wok, then drain on absorbent kitchen paper.

4 Add the red peppers to the wok and stir-fry for 1 minute over a high heat. Add the curry powder or paste and cook for a further 30 seconds, then add the chicken stock, sugar, Chinese rice wine and soy sauce.

5 Mix the remaining cornflour with 1 teaspoon of cold water and add to the wok, stirring. Bring to the boil and simmer gently for 1 minute.

6 Return the chicken to the wok, then simmer for a further 1 minute before adding the rice. Stir over a medium heat for another 2 minutes until heated through. Garnish with the sprigs of coriander and serve.

CHAR SUI PORK & NOODLE SALAD

INGREDIENTS

Serves 4

200 g/7 oz flat rice noodles
4 tbsp black treacle
2 tbsp dark soy sauce
3 tbsp Chinese rice wine or
   dry sherry
3 star anise, roughly crushed
1 cinnamon stick
350 g/12 oz pork tenderloin, in
   1 piece
1 tbsp groundnut oil
2 garlic cloves, peeled and
   finely chopped

1 tsp freshly grated root
   ginger
3 spring onions, trimmed
   and sliced
125 g/4 oz pak choi, roughly
   chopped
2 tbsp light soy sauce
fresh coriander leaves, to
   garnish
prepared or bought plum
   sauce (see page 172),
   to serve

1 Preheat the oven to 220°C/ 425°F/Gas Mark 7, 15 minutes before cooking. Soak the noodles in boiling water according to the packet directions. Drain and reserve. Place the treacle, soy sauce, Chinese rice wine or sherry, star anise and cinnamon into a small saucepan and stir over a gentle heat until mixed thoroughly, then reserve.

2 Trim the pork tenderloin of any excess fat and put into a shallow dish. Pour the cooled sauce over the tenderloin. Turn the pork, making sure it is completely coated in the sauce. Place in the refrigerator and leave to marinate for 4 hours, turning occasionally.

3 Remove the pork from its marinade and transfer to a roasting tin. Roast in the preheated oven for 12–14 minutes, basting once, until the pork is cooked through. Remove from the oven and leave until just warm.

4 Heat the wok, add the oil and when hot, add the garlic, ginger and spring onions. Stir-fry for 30 seconds before adding the pak choi. Stir-fry for a further 1 minute until the pak choi has wilted, then add the noodles and soy sauce. Toss for a few seconds until well mixed, then transfer to a large serving dish. Leave to cool.

5 Thickly slice the pork fillet and add to the cooled noodles. Garnish with coriander leaves and serve with plum sauce.

TASTY TIP

In fine weather, the pork can be cooked on the barbecue for a pleasant smoky flavour.

THAI RICE CAKES WITH MANGO SALSA

INGREDIENTS

Serves 4

225 g/8 oz Thai fragrant rice
400 g can coconut milk
1 lemon grass stalk, bruised
2 kaffir lime leaves, shredded
1 tbsp vegetable oil, plus extra
  for deep frying
1 garlic clove, peeled and
  finely chopped
1 tsp freshly grated root
  ginger
1 red pepper, deseeded and
  finely chopped
2 red chillies, deseeded and
  finely chopped

1 medium egg, beaten
25 g/1 oz dried breadcrumbs

FOR THE MANGO SALSA:
1 large mango, peeled, stoned
  and finely chopped
1 small red onion, peeled and
  finely chopped
2 tbsp freshly chopped
  coriander
2 tbsp freshly chopped basil
juice of 1 lime

1 Wash the rice in several changes of water until the water stays relatively clear. Drain, place in a saucepan with a tight-fitting lid and add the coconut milk, lemon grass and lime leaves. Bring to the boil, cover and cook over the lowest possible heat for 10 minutes. Turn off the heat and leave to stand for 10 minutes, without lifting the lid.

2 Heat the wok, then add 1 tablespoon of oil and when hot, add the garlic, ginger, red pepper and half the chilli. Stir-fry for 1–2 minutes until just softened then place in a large bowl.

3 When the rice is cooked, turn into the mixing bowl

and add the egg. Season to taste with salt and pepper and mix together well. Put the breadcrumbs into a shallow dish. Form the rice mixture into 8 cakes and coat them in the breadcrumbs. Chill the cakes in the refrigerator for 30 minutes.

4 Meanwhile, make the mango salsa. In a bowl, mix together the mango, red onion, coriander, basil, lime juice and remaining red chilli and reserve.

5 Fill a clean wok about one-third full of vegetable oil. Heat to 190°C/375°F, or until a cube of bread browns in 30 seconds. Cook the rice cakes, 1 or 2 at a time, for 2–3 minutes until golden and crisp. Drain on absorbent kitchen paper. Serve with the mango salsa.

FRAGRANT FRUIT PILAF

INGREDIENTS   Serves 4–6

50 g/2 oz butter
6 green cardamom pods
1 cinnamon stick
2 bay leaves
450 g/1 lb basmati rice
600 ml/1 pint chicken stock
1 onion, peeled and finely
  chopped
50 g/2 oz flaked almonds
50 g/2 oz shelled pistachios,
  roughly chopped

125 g/4 oz ready-to-eat dried
  figs, roughly chopped
50 g/2 oz ready-to-eat dried
  apricots, roughly chopped
275 g/10 oz skinless chicken
  breast fillets, cut into chunks
salt and freshly ground black
  pepper
fresh parsley or coriander
  leaves, to garnish

1 Melt half the butter in a saucepan or casserole dish with a tight-fitting lid. Add the cardamom pods and cinnamon stick and cook for about 30 seconds before adding the bay leaves and rice. Stir well to coat the rice in the butter and add the stock. Bring to the boil, cover tightly and cook very gently for 15 minutes. Remove from the heat and leave to stand for a further 5 minutes.

2 Melt the remaining butter in a wok and when foaming, add the onion, flaked almonds and pistachios. Stir-fry for 3–4 minutes until the nuts are beginning to brown. Remove and reserve.

3 Reduce the heat slightly and add the dried figs, apricots and chicken and continue stir-frying for a further 7–8 minutes until the chicken is cooked through. Return the nuts mixture and toss to mix.

4 Remove from the heat, then remove the cinnamon stick and bay leaves. Add the cooked rice and stir together well to mix. Season to taste with salt and pepper. Garnish with parsley or coriander leaves and serve immediately.

TASTY TIP

Leave the chicken out of this recipe, reducing the cooking time accordingly, to make a tasty side dish or vegetarian option.

RICE WITH SQUASH & SAGE

INGREDIENTS

Serves 4–6

450 g/1 lb butternut squash
75 g/3 oz unsalted butter
1 small onion, peeled and
  finely chopped
3 garlic cloves, peeled and
  crushed
2 tbsp freshly chopped
  sage
1 litre/1¾ pints vegetable
  or chicken stock
450 g/1 lb Arborio rice

50 g/2 oz pine nuts, toasted
25 g/1 oz freshly grated
  Parmesan cheese
freshly snipped chives, to
  garnish
salt and freshly ground black
  pepper

1 Peel the squash, cut in half lengthways and remove seeds and stringy flesh. Cut remaining flesh into small cubes and reserve.

2 Heat the wok, add the butter and heat until foaming, then add the onion, garlic and sage and stir-fry for 1 minute.

3 Add the squash to the wok and stir-fry for a further 10–12 minutes, or until the squash is tender. Remove from the heat.

4 Meanwhile, bring the vegetable or chicken stock to the boil and add the rice. Cook for 8–10 minutes, or until the rice is just tender but still quite wet.

5 Add the cooked rice to the squash mixture. Stir in the pine nuts and Parmesan, season to taste with salt and pepper. Garnish with snipped chives and serve immediately.

FOOD FACT

Butternut squash are available most of the year and have a golden skin and a vibrant orange, well-flavoured flesh, which is drier than pumpkin. Use the flesh as directed in the recipe.

BASMATI RICE WITH SAFFRON & BROAD BEANS

INGREDIENTS   Serves 4

1 medium egg
2 tbsp olive oil
1 tbsp freshly chopped mixed
  herbs
salt and freshly ground black
  pepper
200 g/7 oz basmati rice
50 g/2 oz butter
1 small onion, peeled and
  finely chopped

1 garlic clove, peeled and
  finely chopped
large pinch saffron strands
225 g/8 oz shelled broad
  beans, blanched

1 Beat the egg with 1 teaspoon of olive oil and the herbs. Season lightly with salt and pepper. Heat the remaining teaspoon of olive oil in a wok or small frying wok. Pour half the egg mixture into the pan, tilting it to coat the bottom. Cook gently until set on top. Flip over and cook for a further 30 seconds. Transfer to a plate and repeat, using the remaining mixture, then reserve.

2 Wash the rice in several changes of water until the water remains relatively clear. Add the drained rice to a large saucepan of boiling salted water and cook for 12–15 minutes until tender. Drain well and reserve.

3 Heat the butter with the remaining oil in a wok and add the onion and garlic. Cook gently for 3–4 minutes until

the onion is softened. Add the saffron and stir well. Add the drained rice and stir before adding the broad beans. Cook for a further 2–3 minutes, or until heated through.

4 Meanwhile, roll the egg pancakes into cigar shapes then slice crossways into strips. To serve, divide the rice between individual serving bowls and top with the egg strips.

FOOD FACT

Saffron is very expensive and is sold in tiny amounts. It adds a distinctive aroma, a buttery flavour and beautiful colour to food it is cooked with. Before using, crush it lightly in a pestle and mortar.

THAI FRIED RICE WITH PRAWNS & CHILLIES

INGREDIENTS   Serves 4

350 g/12 oz Thai fragrant rice
2 tbsp groundnut or vegetable oil
2 garlic cloves, peeled and finely chopped
2 red chillies, deseeded and finely chopped
125 g/4 oz peeled raw prawns
1 tbsp Thai fish sauce
¼ tsp sugar
1 tbsp light soy sauce

½ small onion, peeled and finely sliced
½ red pepper, deseeded and finely sliced
1 spring onion, green part only, cut into long strips
sprigs of fresh coriander, to garnish

1 Wash the rice in several changes of water until the water remains relatively clear. Drain well. Bring a large saucepan of salted water to the boil and add the rice. Cook for 12–15 minutes until tender. Drain well and reserve.

2 Heat a wok, add the oil and when very hot, add the garlic and stir-fry for 20 seconds, or until just browned. Add the chillies and prawns and stir-fry for 2–3 minutes.

3 Add the fish sauce, sugar and soy sauce and stir-fry for another 30 seconds, or until the prawns are cooked through.

4 Add the cooked rice to the wok and stir together well. Then add the onion, red pepper and spring onion, mix together for a further 1 minute, then turn onto a serving platter. Garnish with sprigs of fresh coriander and serve immediately.

FOOD FACT

Thai fragrant, or jasmine rice is a good-quality long-grain rice with a delicate scent, similar to basmati rice. The rice should be washed in several changes of water until the water remains relatively clear and then drained thoroughly. Cook the rice according to the directions on the packet.

SPICED TOMATO PILAU

INGREDIENTS
Serves 2–3

225 g/8 oz basmati rice
40 g/1½ oz unsalted butter
4 green cardamom pods
2 star anise
4 whole cloves
10 black peppercorns
5 cm/2 inch piece cinnamon
 stick
1 large red onion, peeled and
 finely sliced

175 g/6 oz canned chopped
 tomatoes
salt and freshly ground black
 pepper
sprigs of fresh coriander, to
 garnish

1 Wash the rice in several changes of water until the water remains relatively clear. Drain the rice and cover with fresh water. Leave to soak for 30 minutes. Drain well and reserve.

2 Heat the wok, then melt the butter and add the cardamoms, star anise, cloves, black peppercorns and the cinnamon stick. Cook gently for 30 seconds. Increase the heat and add the onion. Stir-fry for 7–8 minutes until tender and starting to brown. Add the drained rice and cook a further 2–3 minutes.

3 Sieve the tomatoes and mix with sufficient warm water to make 450 ml/16 fl oz. Pour this into the wok, season to taste with salt and pepper and bring to the boil.

4 Cover, reduce the heat to very low and cook for 10 minutes. Remove the wok from the heat and leave covered for a further 10 minutes. Do not lift the lid during cooking or resting. Finally, uncover and mix well with a fork, heat for 1 minute, then garnish with the sprigs of fresh coriander and serve immediately.

HELPFUL HINT

The whole spices in this recipe are not meant to be eaten. Remove them before serving.

CHICKEN WITH NOODLES

INGREDIENTS
Serves 2–3

225 g/8 oz medium egg
noodles

125 g/4 oz skinless, boneless
chicken breast fillets

1 tbsp light soy sauce

2 tsp Chinese rice wine or dry
sherry

5 tsp groundnut oil

2 garlic cloves, peeled and
finely chopped

50 g/2 oz mangetout peas

25 g/1 oz smoked back bacon,
cut into fine strips

½ tsp sugar

2 spring onions, peeled and
finely chopped

1 tsp sesame oil

1 Cook the noodles according to the packet directions. Drain and refresh under cold water. Drain again and reserve.

2 Slice the chicken into fine shreds and mix with 2 teaspoons of the light soy sauce and Chinese rice wine. Leave to marinate in the refrigerator for 10 minutes.

3 Heat a wok, add 2 teaspoons of the oil and when hot, stir-fry the chicken shreds for about 2 minutes, then transfer to a plate. Wipe the wok clean with absorbent kitchen paper.

4 Return the wok to the heat and add the remaining oil. Add the garlic, then after 10 seconds add the mangetout peas and bacon. Stir-fry for a further 1 minute, then add the drained noodles, remaining soy sauce, sugar and spring onions. Stir-fry

for a further 2 minutes then add the reserved chicken.

5 Stir-fry for a further 3–4 minutes until the chicken is cooked through. Add the sesame oil and mix together. Serve either hot or cold.

FOOD FACT

Chow mein literally means 'stir-fried noodles'. There are no hard and fast rules about which meat, fish or vegetables can be used. Chow mein also makes a tasty salad if served cold.

CHINESE BEAN SAUCE NOODLES

INGREDIENTS   Serves 4

250 g/9oz fine egg noodles
1½ tbsp sesame oil
1 tbsp groundnut oil
3 garlic cloves, peeled and
  finely chopped
4 spring onions, trimmed and
  finely chopped
450 g/1 lb fresh pork mince
100 ml/4 fl oz crushed yellow
  bean sauce
1-2 tsp hot chilli sauce

1 tbsp Chinese rice wine or
  dry sherry
2 tbsp dark soy sauce
½ tsp cayenne pepper
2 tsp sugar
150 ml/¼ pint chicken stock

1 Put the noodles into a large bowl and pour over boiling water to cover. Leave to soak according to packet directions until tender. Drain well and place in a bowl with the sesame oil. Toss together well and reserve.

2 Heat a wok until it is hot, add the groundnut oil and when it is hot, add the garlic and half the spring onions. Stir-fry for a few seconds, then add the pork. Stir well to break up and continue to stir-fry for 1–2 minutes until it changes colour.

3 Add the yellow bean sauce, chilli sauce, Chinese rice wine or sherry, soy sauce, cayenne pepper, sugar and chicken stock, stirring all the time. Bring to the boil, reduce the heat and simmer for 5 minutes.

4 Meanwhile, bring a large saucepan of water to the boil and add the noodles for about 20 seconds. Drain well and tip into a warmed serving bowl. Pour the sauce over the top, sprinkle with the remaining spring onions and mix well. Serve immediately.

FOOD FACT

Yellow bean sauce is a thick, spicy sauce made with yellow beans, flour and salt fermented together. It is quite salty but adds a distinctive flavour. Available as whole beans in a thick sauce or as mashed beans (also known as crushed bean sauce). The whole bean sauce tends to be less salty.

BEEF NOODLE SOUP

INGREDIENTS

Serves 4

900 g/2 lb boneless shin or
braising steak
1 cinnamon stick
2 star anise
2 tbsp light soy sauce
6 dried red chillies or 3 fresh,
chopped in half
2 dried citrus peels, soaked
and diced (optional)
1.1 litre/2 pints beef or chicken
stock

350 g/12 oz egg noodles
2 spring onions, trimmed and
chopped, to garnish
warm chunks of crusty
farmhouse bread, to
serve (optional)

1 Trim the meat of any fat and
sinew, then cut into thin
strips. Place the meat, cinnamon,
star anise, soy sauce, red chillies,
chopped citrus peels (if using),
and stock into the wok. Bring to
the boil, then reduce the heat to
a simmer. Skim any fat or scum
that floats to the surface. Cover
the wok and simmer for about
1½ hours or until the meat
is tender.

2 Meanwhile, bring a saucepan
of lightly salted water to the
boil, then add the noodles and
cook in the boiling water for 3–4
minutes until tender or according
to packet directions. Drain well
and reserve.

3 When the meat is tender, add
the noodles to the wok and
simmer for a further 1–2 minutes
until the noodles are heated
through thoroughly. Ladle the
soup into warm shallow soup

bowls or dishes and scatter with
chopped spring onions. Serve,
if liked, with chunks of warm
crusty bread.

HELPFUL HINT

It is important to use shin or
braising steak for this recipe
because of the long cooking
time required. A leaner cut of
meat will end up dry
and chewy.

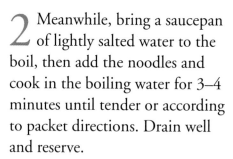

CHICKEN NOODLE SOUP

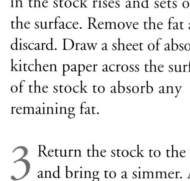

INGREDIENTS Serves 4

carcass of a medium-sized
cooked chicken

1 large carrot, peeled and
roughly chopped

1 medium onion, peeled and
quartered

1 leek, trimmed and roughly
chopped

2–3 bay leaves

a few black peppercorns

2 litres/3½ pints water

225 g/8 oz Chinese cabbage,
trimmed

50 g/2 oz chestnut
mushrooms, wiped and
sliced

125 g/4 oz cooked chicken,
sliced or chopped

50 g/2 oz medium or fine egg
thread noodles

1 Break the chicken carcass into smaller pieces and place in the wok with the carrot, onion, leek, bay leaves, peppercorns and water. Bring slowly to the boil. Skim away any fat or scum that rises for the first 15 minutes. Simmer very gently for 1–1½ hours. If the liquid reduces by more than one third, add a little more water.

2 Remove from the heat and leave until cold. Strain into a large bowl and chill in the refrigerator until any fat in the stock rises and sets on the surface. Remove the fat and discard. Draw a sheet of absorbent kitchen paper across the surface of the stock to absorb any remaining fat.

3 Return the stock to the wok and bring to a simmer. Add the Chinese cabbage, mushrooms and chicken and simmer gently

for 7–8 minutes until the vegetables are tender.

4 Meanwhile, cook the noodles according to the packet directions until tender. Drain well. Transfer a portion of noodles to each serving bowl before pouring in some soup and vegetables. Serve immediately.

HELPFUL HINT

This is an excellent way to
use up any leftover chicken as
well as the carcass from
a roast chicken.

CRISPY NOODLE SALAD

INGREDIENTS
Serves 4

2 tbsp sunflower seeds
2 tbsp pumpkin seeds
50 g/2 oz rice vermicelli or
   stir-fry noodles
175 g/6 oz unsalted butter
2 tbsp sesame seeds,
   lightly toasted
125 g/4 oz red cabbage,
   trimmed and shredded
1 orange pepper, deseeded
   and finely chopped

125 g/4 oz button mushrooms,
   wiped and quartered
2 spring onions, trimmed and
   finely chopped
salt and freshly ground black
   pepper
shredded pickled sushi ginger,
   to garnish

1 Preheat the oven to 200°C/ 400°F/Gas Mark 6, then sprinkle the sunflower and pumpkin seeds on a baking sheet. Toast in the oven, stirring occasionally, for 10–15 minutes or until lightly toasted. Remove from the oven and leave to cool.

2 Crush the rice vermicelli into small pieces (this is easiest in a plastic bag or while the noodles are still in the packet), and reserve. Melt the butter in a small saucepan and leave to cool for a few minutes. Pour the clear yellow liquid carefully into a bowl, leaving behind the white milky solids. Discard the milky solids.

3 Heat the yellow, clarified butter in a wok and fry the crushed noodles in batches until browned, stirring constantly and gently. Remove the fried noodles as they cook, using a slotted spoon, and drain on absorbent

kitchen paper. Transfer the noodles to a bowl and add the toasted seeds.

4 Mix together the red cabbage, orange pepper, button mushrooms and spring onions in a large bowl and season to taste with salt and pepper. Just before serving, add the noodles and seeds to the salad and mix gently. Garnish with a little sushi ginger and serve.

HELPFUL HINT

Do not leave the salad to stand after adding the crispy noodles, as the moisture in the vegetables will cause them to wilt and soften.

THAI SPICY PRAWN & LETTUCE NOODLE SOUP

INGREDIENTS   Serves 4

225 g/8 oz raw tiger prawns
1 tbsp groundnut or vegetable
  oil
2 garlic cloves, peeled and
  crushed
1 red chilli, deseeded and
  finely chopped
1 tbsp freshly grated root
  ginger
4 spring onions, trimmed and
  finely sliced
1.1 litre/2 pints chicken stock

1 kaffir lime leaf, finely
  shredded
1 lemon grass stalk, outer
  leaves discarded and finely
  chopped
75 g/3 oz shiitake mushrooms,
  sliced
125 g/4 oz medium egg thread
  noodles
50 g/2 oz lettuce, shredded
75 g/3 oz beansprouts

1 Peel the prawns, leaving the tail tip on. Cut almost in half down the back of the prawn, discarding any dark veins and open out. Rinse lightly, then pat dry with absorbent kitchen paper and reserve.

2 Heat a wok until very hot, then add the oil and when hot, add the garlic, chilli, ginger and spring onions and stir-fry for 30 seconds. Add the prawns and stir-fry for a further 1 minute.

3 Add the chicken stock, lime leaf and lemon grass and bring to the boil. Reduce the heat and simmer for 10 minutes, adding the mushrooms after 7–8 minutes.

4 Meanwhile, cook the noodles in plenty of boiling water according to the packet directions.

Drain well. Add to the soup with the lettuce and beansprouts and return to the boil; simmer for about 30 seconds. Divide the soup between individual bowls and serve immediately.

FOOD FACT

Kaffir lime leaves are an essential ingredient in Thai cooking and impart a pungent lemon-lime flavour. They are not to be confused with limes, which are grown in Europe, whose leaves are larger and paler in colour. The skin of the kaffir lime itself imparts a similar flavour. Lime leaves are available in Oriental grocers, usually sold in bags or on stalks and they freeze well.

SEAFOOD NOODLE SALAD

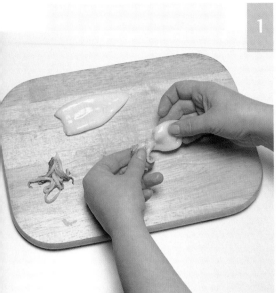

INGREDIENTS

Serves 4

8 baby squid, cleaned
2 tbsp mirin
2 tbsp rice vinegar
4 tbsp sunflower oil
1 red chilli, deseeded and
  finely chopped
2 garlic cloves, peeled and
  crushed
6 spring onions, trimmed
  and finely sliced

1 red pepper, deseeded and
  finely sliced
1 tbsp turmeric
2 tsp ground coriander
8 raw tiger prawns, peeled
175 g/6 oz medium egg noodles
175 g/6 oz fresh white
  crabmeat
50 g/2 oz beansprouts
salt and freshly ground black
  pepper

1 Remove the tentacles from the squid and reserve. Slit the squid bodies open down one side and open out flat.

2 Using a small sharp knife, score the flesh diagonally, first in one direction then the other, to make diamond shapes. Place in a bowl with the squid tentacles, mirin, rice vinegar, half the oil and the chilli and leave to marinate in the refrigerator for 1 hour.

3 Heat a wok until very hot. Add the remaining oil and, when hot, add the garlic, half the spring onions and the red pepper. Stir-fry for 1 minute, then add the turmeric and coriander. Cook for a further 30 seconds before adding the cleaned squid and its marinade and the prawns. Bring to the boil and simmer for 2–3 minutes, or until the squid and prawns are tender. Remove from the heat and leave to cool.

4 Cook the noodles for 3–4 minutes until tender, or according to packet directions. Drain well and put in a large serving bowl along with the white crabmeat and the cooled squid and prawn mixture. Stir together and leave until cold. Just before serving, add the beansprouts and remaining spring onions with seasoning to taste and serve.

HELPFUL HINT

Supermarkets with fresh fish counters usually sell baby squid that is cleaned. If they are not available, buy a large squid weighing about 350 g/12 oz. Have the fishmonger clean it, then treat it in the same way as the baby squid described in step 1. Instead of scoring the flesh, cut it into 5 cm/2 inch squares and cook as above.

CHINESE FRIED RICE

INGREDIENTS   Serves 4

450 g/1 lb long-grain rice
2 tbsp groundnut oil
50 g/2 oz smoked bacon,
  chopped
2 garlic cloves, peeled and
  finely chopped
1 tsp freshly grated root
  ginger
125 g/4 oz frozen peas, thawed
2 medium eggs, beaten
125 g/4 oz beansprouts

salt and freshly ground black
  pepper

TO GARNISH:
50 g/2 oz roasted peanuts,
  chopped
3 spring onions, trimmed and
  finely chopped

1 Wash the rice in several changes of water until it runs relatively clear. Drain well. Put into a saucepan or flameproof casserole dish with a tight-fitting lid. Pour in enough water to cover the rice by about 1 cm/ ½ inch. Add salt and bring to the boil. As soon as the water boils, cover the saucepan, reduce the heat as low as possible and cook for 10 minutes. Remove from the heat and leave to stand for a further 10 minutes. Do not lift the lid while cooking. Leave until cold, then stir with a fork.

2 Heat a wok, add the oil and when hot, add the smoked bacon. Stir-fry for 1 minute before adding the garlic and ginger, then stir-fry for a further 30 seconds.

3 Add the cooked rice and peas to the wok. Stir-fry over a high heat for 5 minutes.

4 Add the eggs and the beansprouts and continue to stir-fry for a further 2 minutes until the eggs have set. Season to taste with salt and pepper. Spoon the mixture onto a serving plate and garnish with the peanuts and spring onions. Serve hot or cold.

TASTY TIP

This dish is an excellent accompaniment to plain grilled chicken or fish or to serve with any meat that has been marinated with Chinese flavours.

HONEY-GLAZED DUCK IN KUMQUAT SAUCE

INGREDIENTS   Serves 4

4 duck breast fillets
1 tbsp light soy sauce
1 tsp sesame oil
1 tbsp clear honey
3 tbsp brandy
1 tbsp sunflower oil
2 tbsp caster sugar
1 tbsp white wine vinegar
150 ml/¼ pint orange juice
125 g/4 oz kumquats, thinly
    sliced

2 tsp cornflour
salt and freshly ground black
    pepper
fresh watercress, to garnish
basmati and wild rice, to serve

1 Thinly slice the duck breasts and put in a shallow bowl. Mix together the soy sauce, sesame oil, honey and 1 tablespoon of brandy. Pour over the duck, stir well, cover and marinate in the refrigerator for at least 1 hour.

2 Heat a wok until hot, add the sunflower oil and swirl it round to coat the sides. Drain the duck, reserving the marinade, and stir-fry over a high heat for 2–3 minutes, or until browned. Remove from the wok; reserve.

3 Wipe the wok clean with absorbent kitchen paper. Add the sugar, vinegar and 1 tablespoon of water. Gently heat until the sugar dissolves, then boil until a rich golden colour. Pour in the orange juice, then the remaining brandy. Stir in the kumquat slices and simmer for 5 minutes.

4 Blend the cornflour with 1 tablespoon of cold water. Add to the wok and simmer for 2–3 minutes, stirring until thickened. Return the duck to the wok and cook gently for 1–2 minutes, or until warmed through. Season to taste with salt and pepper. Spoon onto warmed plates and garnish with fresh watercress leaves. Serve immediately with freshly cooked basmati and wild rice.

FOOD FACT

Kumquats are tiny citrus fruits that resemble miniature oranges. They have a strong sharp/sweet flavour and are entirely edible, skin and all. They often contain many seeds, so it is worth halving or slicing them before using.

APPLE-TOSSED PORK

INGREDIENTS

Serves 4

350 g/12 oz pork fillet
2 tbsp plain flour
salt and freshly ground black pepper
1½ tbsp sunflower oil
15 g/½ oz unsalted butter
2 dessert apples, peeled, cored and thinly sliced
2 tsp Dijon mustard
1 tbsp freshly chopped sage
2 tbsp Calvados brandy

4 tbsp crème fraîche
fresh sage leaves, to garnish
freshly cooked beans, to serve

1 Trim away any visible fat from the pork fillet, then cut across into 1 cm/½ inch thick slices. Season the flour, then add the pork slices a few at a time and toss until lightly coated.

2 Heat a wok, then add the oil and heat. Stir-fry the meat in 2 batches over a fairly high heat until well browned. Remove from the wok and reserve.

3 Melt the butter in the wok, add the apple slices and cook, stirring all the time, for 1 minute. Stir in the mustard, chopped sage, Calvados brandy and crème fraîche. Bring to the boil, stirring.

4 Return the pork and any juices to the wok and cook over a gentle heat for 1–2 minutes, or until the meat has warmed though, the apples are just tender and the sauce is bubbling. Spoon onto warmed plates, garnish with fresh sage leaves and serve immediately with freshly cooked green beans.

TASTY TIP

For an easy braised red cabbage recipe to serve with the pork, thinly slice 1 onion and 450 g/1 lb red cabbage. Heat 2 tablespoons vegetable or olive oil in a large saucepan and add the onion and cabbage along with 1 teaspoon of caraway seeds. Cook very gently, stirring occasionally, for 10 minutes. Then add 150 ml/¼ pint vegetable or chicken stock, cover and simmer gently for about 1–1½ hours or until tender, adding a little extra stock or water if necessary.

MIXED CANAPÉS

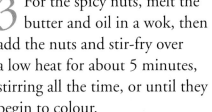

INGREDIENTS   Serves 12

FOR THE STIR-FRIED CHEESE CANAPÉS:

6 thick slices white bread
40 g/1½ oz butter, softened
75 g/3 oz mature Cheddar, cheese grated
75 g/3 oz blue cheese such as Stilton or Gorgonzola, crumbled
3 tbsp sunflower oil

FOR THE SPICY NUTS:

25 g/1 oz unsalted butter
2 tbsp light olive oil
450 g/1 lb mixed unsalted nuts
1 tsp ground paprika
½ tsp ground cumin
½ tsp fine sea salt
sprigs of fresh coriander, to garnish

1 For the cheese canapés, cut the crusts off the bread, then gently roll with a rolling pin to flatten slightly. Thinly spread with butter, then sprinkle over the mixed cheeses as evenly as possible.

2 Roll up each slice tightly, then cut into 4 slices, each about 2.5 cm/1 inch long. Heat the oil in a wok or large frying pan and stir-fry the cheese rolls in 2 batches, turning them all the time until golden brown and crisp. Drain on absorbent kitchen paper and serve warm or cold.

3 For the spicy nuts, melt the butter and oil in a wok, then add the nuts and stir-fry over a low heat for about 5 minutes, stirring all the time, or until they begin to colour.

4 Sprinkle the paprika and cumin over the nuts and continue stir-frying for a further 1–2 minutes, or until the nuts are golden brown.

5 Remove from the wok and drain on absorbent kitchen paper. Sprinkle with the salt, garnish with sprigs of fresh coriander and serve hot or cold. If serving cold, store both the cheese canapés and the spicy nuts in airtight containers.

TASTY TIP

These canapés are perfect for serving at a buffet or finger food party, or you can halve the quantities and serve with drinks instead of a starter at an informal dinner party for 4–6 people.

KUNG-PAO LAMB

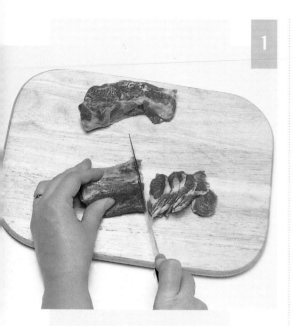

INGREDIENTS   Serves 4

450 g/1 lb lamb fillet
2 tbsp soy sauce
2 tbsp Chinese rice wine or
  dry sherry
2 tbsp sunflower oil
2 tsp sesame oil
50 g/2 oz unsalted peanuts
1 garlic clove, peeled and
  crushed
2.5 cm/1 inch piece fresh root
  ginger, finely chopped
1 red chilli, deseeded and
  finely chopped

1 small green pepper,
  deseeded and diced
6 spring onions, trimmed and
  diagonally sliced
125 ml/4 fl oz lamb or
  vegetable stock
1 tsp red wine vinegar
1 tsp soft light brown sugar
2 tsp cornflour
plain boiled or steamed white
  rice, to serve

1 Wrap the lamb in baking parchment paper and place in the freezer for about 30 minutes until stiff. Cut the meat across the grain into paper-thin slices. Put in a shallow bowl, add 2 teaspoons of the soy sauce and all the Chinese rice wine or sherry and leave to marinate in the refrigerator for 15 minutes.

2 Heat a wok or frying pan until hot, add the sunflower oil and swirl it around to coat the sides. Add the lamb and stir-fry for about 1 minute until lightly browned. Remove from the wok or pan and reserve, leaving any juices behind.

3 Add the sesame oil to the wok or pan and stir-fry the peanuts, garlic, ginger, chilli, green pepper and spring onions for 1–2 minutes, or until the nuts are golden. Return the lamb with the remaining soy sauce, stock, vinegar and sugar.

4 Blend the cornflour with 1 tablespoon of water. Stir in and cook the mixture for 1–2 minutes, or until the vegetables are tender and the sauce has thickened. Serve immediately with plain boiled or steamed white rice.

FOOD FACT

No-one knows exactly who Kung-Pao was; some believe he was an emperor, others a famous cook – only this famous and delicious stir-fry remains as a tribute.

PRAWN SPECIAL FRIED RICE

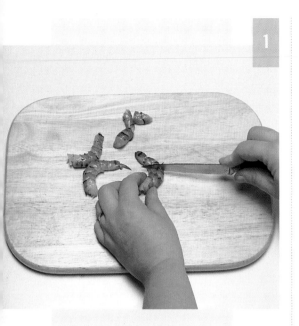

INGREDIENTS

Serves 4

225 g/8 oz raw prawns, peeled
2 tbsp light soy sauce
1 tsp caster sugar
2.5 cm/1 inch piece fresh root
  ginger, peeled and grated
4 medium eggs
pinch of salt
1 tbsp freshly chopped
  coriander
2 tbsp freshly chopped parsley
3 tbsp sunflower oil

1 bunch spring onions,
  trimmed and finely sliced
350 g/12 oz cooked long-grain
  rice
50 g/2 oz frozen peas, thawed
freshly ground black pepper

1 Using a small, sharp knife, remove the thin black thread that runs down the back of the prawns, then rinse and pat dry with absorbent kitchen paper. Chop in half or thirds, then place in a bowl with the soy sauce, sugar and ginger. Mix well and reserve.

2 Whisk together 2 of the eggs with salt and the chopped coriander and parsley. Heat 1 tablespoon of the oil in a wok over a low heat and pour in the egg mixture. Tilt the wok so the mixture spreads to an even layer.

3 Cook gently, stirring, until the mixture begins to set, then stop stirring and cook for a further 30 seconds until the underneath is golden brown and the top is still slightly creamy. Tip the omelette onto a clean chopping board and leave to cool. When cold, roll up loosely and cut into fine slices. Wipe the wok clean.

4 Heat the remaining oil and stir-fry the prawns for 2–3 minutes, or until they are cooked and have turned pink. Add the spring onions and continue stir-frying for a further 1–2 minutes.

5 Add the rice and peas and stir-fry for 2 minutes. Lightly beat the remaining 2 eggs. Drizzle over the rice, then stir-fry for about 30 seconds until scrambled. Serve immediately, sprinkled with the shredded omelette.

TASTY TIP

Using raw prawns gives this dish a freshness that cooked prawns would not. They have a much better texture and shrink far less than their cooked counterparts.

CREAMY CHICKEN STROGANOFF

INGREDIENTS

Serves 4

450 g/1 lb skinless chicken
  breast fillets
4 tbsp dry sherry
15 g/½ oz dried porcini
  mushrooms
2 tbsp sunflower oil
25 g/1 oz unsalted butter
1 onion, peeled and sliced
225 g/8 oz chestnut
  mushrooms, wiped and
  sliced
1 tbsp paprika

1 tsp freshly chopped thyme
125 ml/4 fl oz chicken stock
150 ml/¼ pint crème fraîche
salt and freshly ground black
  pepper
sprigs of fresh thyme, to
  garnish

TO SERVE:
crème fraîche
freshly cooked rice or
  egg noodles

1 Cut the chicken into finger-length strips and reserve. Gently warm the sherry in a small saucepan and remove from the heat. Add the porcini mushrooms and leave to soak while preparing the rest of the stir-fry.

2 Heat a wok, add 1½ tablespoons of the oil and when hot, add the chicken and stir-fry over a high heat for 3–4 minutes, or until lightly browned. Remove from the wok and reserve.

3 Heat the remaining oil and butter in the wok and gently cook the onion for 5 minutes. Add the chestnut mushrooms and stir-fry for a further 5 minutes, or until tender. Sprinkle in the paprika and thyme and cook for 30 seconds.

4 Add the porcini mushrooms with their soaking liquid, then stir in the stock and return

the chicken to the wok. Cook for 1–2 minutes, or until the chicken is cooked through and tender.

5 Stir in the crème fraîche and heat until piping hot. Season to taste with salt and pepper. Garnish with sprigs of fresh thyme and serve immediately with a spoonful of crème fraîche and rice or egg noodles.

HELPFUL HINT

Dried porcini mushrooms should be soaked in very hot, but not boiling water for at least 20 minutes. Use the soaking liquor as well as the rehydrated mushrooms in order to obtain maximum flavour from the mushrooms.

QUICK MEDITERRANEAN PRAWNS

INGREDIENTS

Serves 4

20 raw Mediterranean prawns
3 tbsp olive oil
1 garlic clove, peeled and
   crushed
finely grated zest and juice of
   ½ lemon
sprigs of fresh rosemary

**FOR THE PESTO & SUN-
DRIED TOMATO DIPS:**
150 ml/¼ pint Greek style
   yogurt
1 tbsp prepared pesto
150 ml/¼ pint crème fraîche
1 tbsp sun-dried tomato paste
1 tbsp wholegrain mustard
salt and freshly ground black
   pepper
lemon wedges, to garnish

1 Remove the shells from the prawns, leaving the tail shells. Using a small, sharp knife, remove the dark vein that runs along the back of the prawns. Rinse and drain on absorbent kitchen paper.

2 Whisk 2 tablespoons of the oil with the garlic, lemon zest and juice in a small bowl. Bruise 1 sprig of rosemary with a rolling pin and add to the bowl. Add the prawns, toss to coat, then cover and leave to marinate in the refrigerator until needed.

3 For the simple dips, mix the yogurt and pesto in one bowl and the crème fraîche, tomato paste and mustard in another bowl. Season to taste with salt and pepper.

4 Heat a wok, add the remaining oil and swirl round to coat the sides. Remove

the prawns from the marinade, leaving any juices and the rosemary behind. Add to the wok and stir-fry over a high heat for 3–4 minutes, or until the prawns are pink and just cooked through.

5 Remove the prawns from the wok and arrange on a platter. Garnish with lemon wedges and more fresh rosemary sprigs and serve hot or cold with the dips.

HELPFUL HINT

The prawns must be cooked thoroughly, but take care not to overcook them or they will be tough. Remove from the refrigerator and leave at room temperature for 15 minutes before stir-frying.

SWEET-&-SOUR SHREDDED BEEF

INGREDIENTS   Serves 4

350 g/12 oz rump steak
1 tsp sesame oil
2 tbsp Chinese rice wine or
  sweet sherry
2 tbsp dark soy sauce
1 tsp cornflour
4 tbsp pineapple juice
2 tsp soft light brown sugar
1 tsp sherry vinegar
salt and freshly ground black
  pepper
2 tbsp groundnut oil

2 medium carrots, peeled and
  cut into matchsticks
125 g/4 oz mangetout peas,
  trimmed and cut into
  matchsticks
1 bunch spring onions,
  trimmed and shredded
2 garlic cloves, peeled and
  crushed
1 tbsp toasted sesame seeds
freshly cooked Thai fragrant
  rice, to serve

1 Cut the steak across the grain into thin strips. Put in a bowl with the sesame oil, 1 tablespoon of the Chinese rice wine or sherry and 1 tablespoon of the soy sauce. Mix well, cover and leave to marinate in the refrigerator for 30 minutes.

2 In a small bowl, blend together the cornflour with the remaining Chinese rice wine or sherry, then stir in the pineapple juice, remaining soy sauce, sugar and vinegar. Season with a little salt and pepper and reserve.

3 Heat a wok until hot, add 1 tablespoon of the oil, then drain the beef, reserving the marinade, and stir-fry for 1–2 minutes, or until browned. Remove from the wok and reserve.

4 Add the remaining oil to the wok then add the carrots and stir-fry for 1 minute, then add the mangetout peas and spring onions and stir-fry for a further 1 minute.

5 Return the beef to the wok with the sauce, reserved marinade and garlic. Continue cooking for 1 minute or until the vegetables are tender and the sauce is bubbling. Turn the stir-fry into a warmed serving dish, sprinkle with toasted sesame seeds and serve immediately with the Thai fragrant rice.

HELPFUL HINT

It is important to slice the beef across the grain so that it will hold together when it is being cooked.

VEGETABLE KOFTA CURRY

INGREDIENTS   Serves 6

350 g/12 oz potatoes, peeled and diced

225 g/8 oz carrots, peeled and roughly chopped

225 g/8 oz parsnips, peeled and roughly chopped

1 medium egg, lightly beaten

75 g/3 oz plain flour, sifted

8 tbsp sunflower oil

2 onions, peeled and sliced

2 garlic cloves, peeled and crushed

2.5 cm/1 inch piece fresh root ginger, peeled and grated

2 tbsp garam masala

2 tbsp tomato paste

300 ml/½ pint vegetable stock

250 ml/9 fl oz Greek style yogurt

3 tbsp freshly chopped coriander

salt and freshly ground black pepper

1 Bring a saucepan of lightly salted water to the boil. Add the potatoes, carrots and parsnips. Cover and simmer for 12–15 minutes, or until the vegetables are tender. Drain the vegetables and mash until very smooth. Stir the egg into the vegetable purée, then add the flour and mix to make a stiff paste and reserve.

2 Heat 2 tablespoons of the oil in a wok and gently cook the onions for 10 minutes. Add the garlic and ginger and cook for a further 2–3 minutes, or until very soft and just beginning to colour.

3 Sprinkle the garam masala over the onions and stir in. Add the tomato paste and stock. Bring to the boil, cover and simmer gently for 15 minutes.

4 Meanwhile, heat the remaining oil in a wok or frying pan. Drop in tablespoons of vegetable batter, 4 or 5 at a time and fry, turning often, for 3-4 minutes until brown and crisp. Remove with a slotted spoon and drain on absorbent kitchen paper. Keep warm in a low oven while cooking the rest.

5 Stir the yogurt and coriander into the onion sauce. Slowly heat to boiling point and season to taste with salt and pepper. Divide the koftas between warmed serving plates and spoon over the sauce. Serve immediately.

FOOD FACT

Greek yogurt is made by straining the excess watery liquid from ordinary yogurt, making it thicker and higher in fat than natural yogurt.

BRANDIED BEEF

INGREDIENTS
Serves 4

450 g/1 lb rump steak
2 tsp dark soy sauce
1 tsp soft dark brown sugar
salt and freshly ground black
 pepper
1 small fennel bulb
1 red pepper
1 orange
2 tbsp sunflower oil
15 g/½ oz unsalted butter

225 g/8 oz tiny whole button
 mushrooms
5 tbsp beef stock
3 tbsp brandy
orange wedges, to garnish
freshly cooked rice or noodles,
 to serve

1 Trim any fat from the steak and cut across the grain into thin strips. Place in a shallow bowl with the soy sauce, sugar and a little salt and pepper. Mix well and leave to marinate while preparing the vegetables.

2 Trim the fennel and slice as thinly as possible, from the stems down through the root. Quarter, deseed and thinly slice the red pepper. Thinly pare the rind from about half the orange and cut into fine matchsticks. Squeeze out the juice.

3 Heat the oil and butter in a wok, add the beef and stir-fry for 2 minutes, until brown and tender. Remove with a slotted spoon and reserve.

4 Add the fennel, red pepper and mushrooms to the wok and stir-fry for 3–4 minutes, or until softened. Add the orange zest and juice and the stock and cook for 2 minutes until the sauce is reduced slightly. Return the beef to the wok and stir-fry for 30 seconds to heat through.

5 Heat the brandy in a small saucepan or ladle, ignite, then let the flames subside and pour over the vegetables and meat. Gently shake the wok occasionally until the flames subside. Garnish with a few orange wedges and serve immediately with rice or noodles.

HELPFUL HINT

If you prefer not to flame the brandy in the wok, simply simmer gently for about 5 minutes until the alcohol has evaporated, by which time it will have imparted its flavour to the food.

GARLIC MUSHROOMS WITH CRISPY BACON & CHICKEN LIVER SAUTÉ

INGREDIENTS   Serves 4

4 large field mushrooms

40 g/1½ oz butter, melted and
  cooled

2 garlic cloves, peeled and
  crushed

1 tbsp sunflower oil

3 rashers smoked streaky
  bacon, derinded and
  chopped

4 shallots, peeled and thinly
  sliced

450 g/1 lb chicken livers,
  halved

2 tbsp marsala or sweet sherry

4 tbsp chicken or vegetable
  stock

6 tbsp double cream

2 tsp freshly chopped thyme

salt and freshly ground black
  pepper

1 Remove the stalks from the mushrooms and roughly chop. Mix together 25 g/1 oz of the butter and garlic and brush over both sides of the mushroom caps. Place on the rack of a grill pan.

2 Heat a wok, add the oil and when hot, add the bacon and stir-fry for 2–3 minutes, or until crispy. Remove and reserve. Add the remaining butter to the wok and stir-fry the shallots and chopped mushroom stalks for 4–5 minutes until they are softened.

3 Add the chicken livers and cook for 3–4 minutes, or until well browned on the outside, but still pink and tender inside. Pour in the marsala or sherry and the stock. Simmer for 1 minute, then stir in the cream, thyme, salt and pepper and half

the bacon. Cook for about 30 seconds to heat through.

4 While the livers are frying, cook the mushroom caps under a hot grill for 3–4 minutes each side, until tender.

5 Place the mushrooms on warmed serving plates, allowing 1 per person. Spoon the chicken livers over and around the mushrooms. Scatter with the remaining bacon and serve immediately.

FOOD FACT

This dish makes a wonderful starter for a dinner party or can be served with plain boiled or steamed rice and a green vegetable for an informal supper.

CHICKEN WRAPS

INGREDIENTS   Serves 4

FOR THE STIR-FRIED CHICKEN:
4 skinless chicken breast fillets
finely grated zest and juice of
    1 lime
1 tbsp caster sugar
2 tsp dried oregano
½ tsp ground cinnamon
¼ tsp cayenne pepper
3 tbsp sunflower oil
2 onions, peeled and sliced
1 green, 1 red and 1 yellow
    pepper, deseeded and sliced

salt and freshly ground black
    pepper

FOR THE TORTILLAS:
250 g/9 oz plain flour
pinch of salt
¼ tsp baking powder
50 g/2 oz white vegetable fat

TO SERVE:
soured cream
guacamole

1 Slice the chicken across the grain into 2 cm/¾ inch wide strips. Place in a bowl with the lime zest and juice, sugar, oregano, cinnamon and cayenne pepper. Mix well and leave to marinate while making the tortillas.

2 Sift the flour, salt and baking powder into a bowl. Rub in the white fat, then sprinkle over 4 tablespoons of warm water and mix to a stiff dough. Knead on a lightly floured surface for 10 minutes until smooth and elastic.

3 Divide the dough into 12 equal pieces and roll out each to a 15 cm/6 inch circle. Cover with clingfilm to prevent them drying out before you cook them.

4 Heat a non-stick wok and cook each tortilla for about 1 minute on each side, or until

golden and slightly blistered. Remove the tortillas and keep them warm and pliable in a clean tea towel.

5 Heat 2 tablespoons of the oil in the wok and stir-fry the onions for 5 minutes until lightly coloured. Remove with a slotted spoon and reserve.

6 Add the remaining oil to the wok and heat. Drain the chicken from the marinade and add it to the wok. Stir-fry for 5 minutes, then return the onions, add the pepper slices and cook for a further 3–4 minutes, or until the chicken is cooked through and the vegetables are tender. Season to taste with salt and pepper and serve immediately with the tortillas, soured cream and guacamole.

SESAME-COATED TURKEY WITH MANGO TABBOULEH

INGREDIENTS   Serves 4

3 turkey breast fillets, about
  450 g/1 lb, skinned
4 tbsp plain flour
4 tbsp sesame seeds
salt and freshly ground black
  pepper
1 medium egg, lightly beaten
2 tbsp sunflower oil

**FOR THE MANGO
TABBOULEH:**
175 g/6 oz bulgar wheat
2 tbsp olive oil
juice of ½ lemon
6 spring onions, trimmed and
  finely chopped
1 red chilli, deseeded and
  finely chopped
1 ripe mango, peeled, pitted
  and diced
3 tbsp freshly chopped
  coriander
1 tbsp freshly chopped mint
  leaves

1 Cut the turkey across the grain into strips. Mix together the flour, sesame seeds, salt and pepper. Dip the turkey strips in the beaten egg, then in the sesame seed mixture to coat. Chill in the refrigerator until ready to cook.

2 For the tabbouleh, put the bulgar wheat in a large bowl and pour over plenty of boiling water. Cover the bowl with a plate and leave to soak for 20 minutes.

3 Whisk together the olive oil and lemon juice in a large bowl. Stir in the spring onions, chilli, mango, coriander and mint. Drain the bulgar and squeeze out any excess moisture with your hands, then add to the bowl, season to taste with salt and pepper and mix well.

4 Heat a wok, add the oil and, when hot, stir-fry the sesame-coated turkey strips in 2 batches for 4–5 minutes, or until golden, crispy and cooked through. Divide the turkey strips between individual serving plates and serve immediately with the tabbouleh.

FOOD FACT

Bulgar wheat, sometimes called cracked wheat, is a common ingredient in Middle Eastern cookery. It has a nutty flavour and a firm texture and is equally delicious hot or cold.

SALMON TERIYAKI WITH NOODLES & CRISPY GREENS

INGREDIENTS — Serves 4

350 g/12 oz salmon fillet
3 tbsp Japanese soy sauce
3 tbsp mirin or sweet sherry
3 tbsp sake
1 tbsp freshly grated root ginger
225 g/8 oz spring greens
groundnut oil for deep-frying
pinch of salt
½ tsp caster sugar
125 g/4 oz cellophane noodles

TO GARNISH:
1 tbsp freshly chopped dill
sprigs of fresh dill
zest of ½ lemon

1 Cut the salmon into paper-thin slices and place in a shallow dish. Mix together the soy sauce, mirin or sherry, sake and the ginger. Pour over the salmon, cover and leave to marinate for 15–30 minutes.

2 Remove and discard the thick stalks from the spring greens. Lay several leaves on top of each other, roll up tightly, then shred finely.

3 Pour in enough oil to cover about 5 cm/2 inches of the wok. Deep-fry the greens in batches for about 1 minute each until crisp. Remove and drain on absorbent kitchen paper. Transfer to a serving dish, sprinkle with salt and sugar and toss together.

4 Place the noodles in a bowl and pour over warm water to cover. Leave to soak for 15–20 minutes until soft, then drain. With scissors cut into 15 cm/ 6 inch lengths.

5 Preheat the grill. Remove the salmon slices from the marinade, reserving the marinade for later, and arrange them in a single layer on a baking sheet. Grill for about 2 minutes, until lightly cooked, without turning.

6 When the oil in the wok is cool enough, tip most of it away, leaving about 1 tablespoon behind. Heat until hot, then add the noodles and the reserved marinade and stir-fry for 3–4 minutes. Tip the noodles into a large warmed serving bowl and arrange the salmon slices on top, garnished with chopped dill, sprigs of fresh dill and lemon zest. Scatter with a little of the crispy greens and serve the rest separately.

CHICKEN TIKKA MASALA

INGREDIENTS

Serves 4

4 skinless chicken breast fillets
150 ml/¼ pint natural yogurt
1 garlic clove, peeled and
   crushed
2.5 cm/1 inch piece fresh root
   ginger, peeled and grated
1 tsp chilli powder
1 tbsp ground coriander
2 tbsp lime juice
twist of lime, to garnish
freshly cooked rice, to serve

FOR THE MASALA SAUCE:
15 g/½ oz unsalted butter
2 tbsp sunflower oil
1 onion, peeled and chopped
1 green chilli, deseeded and
   finely chopped
1 tsp garam masala
150 ml/¼ pint double cream
salt and freshly ground black
   pepper
3 tbsp fresh coriander leaves,
   roughly torn

1 Preheat the oven to 200°C/ 400°F/Gas Mark 6, 15 minutes before cooking. Cut each chicken breast across into 3 pieces, then make 2 or 3 shallow cuts in each piece. Put in a shallow dish. Mix together the yogurt, garlic, ginger, chilli powder, ground coriander and lime juice. Pour over the chicken, cover and marinate in the refrigerator for up to 24 hours.

2 Remove the chicken from the marinade and arrange on an oiled baking tray. Bake in the preheated oven for 15 minutes, or until golden brown and cooked.

3 While the chicken is cooking, heat the butter and oil in a wok and stir-fry the onion for 5 minutes, or until tender. Add the chilli and garam masala and stir-fry for a few more seconds. Stir in the cream and remaining

marinade. Simmer over a low heat for 1 minute, stirring all the time.

4 Add the chicken pieces and cook for a further 1 minute, stirring to coat in the sauce. Season to taste with salt and pepper. Transfer the chicken pieces to a warmed serving plate. Stir the chopped coriander into the sauce, then spoon over the chicken, garnish and serve immediately with freshly cooked rice.

TASTY TIP

Make your own garam masala by grinding together ½ teaspoon cardamom seeds, 2.5 cm/1 inch cinnamon stick, ½ teaspoon cumin seeds, ½ teaspoon cloves, ½ teaspoon black peppercorns and 5 gratings of nutmeg, until fine.

MAPLE PEARS WITH PISTACHIOS & SIMPLE CHOCOLATE SAUCE

INGREDIENTS   Serves 4

25 g/1 oz unsalted butter
50 g/2 oz unsalted pistachios
4 medium-ripe firm pears,
    peeled, quartered and cored
2 tsp lemon juice
pinch of ground ginger
    (optional)
6 tbsp maple syrup

FOR THE CHOCOLATE SAUCE:
150 ml/¼ pint double cream
2 tbsp milk
½ tsp vanilla essence
150 g/5 oz plain dark
    chocolate, broken into
    squares and roughly
    chopped

1 Melt the butter in a wok over a medium heat until sizzling. Turn down the heat a little, add the pistachios and stir-fry for 30 seconds.

2 Add the pears to the wok and continue cooking for about 2 minutes, turning frequently and carefully, until the nuts are beginning to brown and the pears are tender.

3 Add the lemon juice, ground ginger if using, and maple syrup. Cook for 3–4 minutes, or until the syrup has reduced slightly. Spoon the pears and the syrup into a serving dish and leave to cool for 1–2 minutes while making the chocolate sauce.

4 Pour the cream and milk into the wok. Add the vanilla essence and heat just to boiling point. Remove the wok from the heat.

5 Add the chocolate to the wok and leave for 1 minute to melt, then stir until the chocolate is evenly mixed with the cream. Pour into a jug and serve while still warm, with the pears.

FOOD FACT

Maple syrup is made by tapping maple trees in early spring when the sap is running. The thin clear liquid is boiled until brown and syrupy. Most commerical syrups are uniform in flavour and colour, but it is possible to find syrups made at later stages in the spring, with a richer character.

TIPSY TROPICAL FRUIT

INGREDIENTS

Serves 4

225 g/8 oz can pineapple
   chunks in natural juice
2 guavas
1 papaya
2 passion fruit
25 g/1 oz unsalted butter
1 tbsp orange juice
50 g/2 oz creamed coconut,
   chopped
50 g/2 oz soft light brown
   sugar

2 tbsp malibu liqueur or white
   rum
sprigs of fresh mint, to
   decorate
vanilla ice-cream, to serve

1 Drain the pineapple chunks, reserving the juice. Pat the pineapple dry on absorbent kitchen paper. Peel the guavas and cut into wedges. Halve the papaya and scoop out the black seeds. Peel and cut into 2.5 cm/ 1 inch chunks. Halve the passion fruit and scoop out the seeds into a small bowl.

2 Heat the butter in a wok, add the pineapple and stir-fry over a high heat for 30 seconds. Turn down the heat and add the guavas and papaya. Drizzle over the orange juice and cook for 2 minutes, stirring occasionally, taking care not to break up the fruit.

3 Using a slotted spoon, remove the fruit from the wok, leaving any juices behind and transfer to a warmed serving dish. Add the creamed coconut to the wok with the sugar and pineapple juice. Simmer for 2–3 minutes, stirring until the coconut has melted.

4 Add the malibu or white rum to the wok and heat through, then pour over the fruit. Spoon the passion fruit pulp on top and serve hot with spoonfuls of ice-cream decorated with a sprig of mint.

FOOD FACT

Passion fruit are small, round, purplish fruits which are ripe when the skin is dimpled and wrinkled. To use them, it is necessary to slice them across the middle and scoop out the seeds and flesh. The seeds are edible and have a lot of flavour, but can be sieved out if preferred.

FRUITED FRENCH TOAST

INGREDIENTS   Serves 4

8 slices spicy fruit loaf, about
   1 cm/½ inch thick
200 ml/7 fl oz milk
3 tbsp orange liqueur
2 medium egg yolks
¼ tsp ground cinnamon
50 g/2 oz unsalted
   butter
1 tbsp sunflower oil
5 tbsp seedless raspberry jam
   or conserve

**FOR THE ORANGE-SCENTED
  CREAM:**
150 ml/¼ pint whipping cream
1 tsp icing sugar
finely grated zest of ½ orange
1 tbsp orange flower water

1 Cut the crusts off the bread, then cut each slice diagonally into 4 triangles. Mix together half the milk and 2 tablespoons of the liqueur. Quickly dip the bread triangles in the mixture, then place on a wire rack over a tray to drain.

2 Beat together the egg yolks, cinnamon, remaining milk and any liqueur-flavoured milk on the tray. Dip the triangles in the egg and return to the rack.

3 Heat half the butter and the oil in a wok. Add the bread triangles about 3 at a time and fry on both sides until well browned. Remove and keep warm in a low oven, while cooking the rest.

4 When needed, add the remaining butter and finish cooking the bread triangles. Add to those keeping warm in the oven while making the sauce.

5 Gently heat the jam in the wok with the remaining 1 tablespoon of liqueur and 1 tablespoon of water until melted, then cook for 1 minute.

6 To make the orange-scented cream, whisk the cream, icing sugar, orange zest and orange flower water together until soft peaks form. Serve the French toasts drizzled with the jam sauce and accompanied by the orange-scented cream.

HELPFUL HINT

The hot butter needs to be watched carefully in between batches. It may go brown, which will add a pleasant nutty flavour, but it is important to make sure that it does not burn.

HOT CHERRY FRITTERS

INGREDIENTS   Serves 6

50 g/2 oz butter
pinch of salt
2 tbsp caster sugar
125 g/4 oz plain flour,
 sifted
¼ tsp ground cinnamon
25 g/1 oz ground almonds
3 medium eggs, lightly beaten
175 g/6 oz cherries, stoned

sunflower oil for frying
2 tbsp icing sugar
1 tsp cocoa powder
sprigs of fresh mint,
 to decorate

1 Place the butter, salt and sugar in a small saucepan with 225 ml/8 fl oz water. Heat gently until the butter has melted, then add the flour and ground cinnamon and beat over a low heat until the mixture leaves the sides of the pan.

2 Remove the saucepan from the heat and beat in the ground almonds. Gradually add the eggs, beating well after each addition. Finally stir in the cherries.

3 Pour 5 cm/2 inches depth of oil in a wok and heat until it reaches 180°C/350°F on a sugar thermometer. Drop in heaped teaspoons of the mixture, cooking 4 or 5 at a time for about 2 minutes, or until lightly browned and crisp.

4 Remove the fritters from the pan with a slotted spoon and drain on absorbent kitchen paper. Keep warm in a low oven while cooking the remaining fritters. Arrange on a warmed serving plate and dust with the icing sugar and cocoa powder. Decorate with mint sprigs and serve hot.

HELPFUL HINT

It is essential to bring the oil back up to temperature each time before cooking the next batch of fritters.

STIR-FRIED BANANAS & PEACHES WITH RUM BUTTERSCOTCH SAUCE

INGREDIENTS

Serves 4

2 medium-firm bananas
1 tbsp caster sugar
2 tsp lime juice
4 firm, ripe peaches or
  nectarines
1 tbsp sunflower oil

**FOR THE RUM
BUTTERSCOTCH SAUCE:**
50 g/2 oz unsalted butter
50 g/2 oz soft light brown
  sugar
125 g/4 oz demerara sugar
300 ml/½ pint double cream
2 tbsp dark rum

1 Peel the bananas and cut into 2.5 cm/1 inch diagonal slices. Place in a bowl and sprinkle with the caster sugar and lime juice and stir until lightly coated. Reserve.

2 Place the peaches or nectarines in a large bowl and pour over boiling water to cover. Leave for 30 seconds, then plunge them into cold water and peel off their skins. Cut each one into 8 thick slices, discarding the stone.

3 Heat a wok, add the oil and swirl it round the wok to coat the sides. Add the fruit and cook for 3–4 minutes, shaking the wok and gently turning the fruit until lightly browned. Spoon the fruit into a warmed serving bowl and clean the wok with absorbent kitchen paper.

4 Add the butter and sugars to the wok and stir continuously over a very low heat until the sugar has dissolved. Remove from the heat and leave to cool for 2–3 minutes.

5 Stir the cream and rum into the sugar syrup and return to the heat. Bring to the boil and simmer for 2 minutes, stirring continuously until smooth. Leave for 2–3 minutes to cool slightly, then serve warm with the stir-fried peaches and bananas.

HELPFUL HINT

Bananas should not be prepared too far ahead of cooking as they tend to discolour. If necessary, dip them in a little lemon juice to stop them turning brown.

INDEX